I0155684

Thunderhorse
25

One Man's Journey
Through Vietnam

By Doug Eggerth

Learn more about this book
and its author by visiting our website:
www.overboardministries.com

Copyright © 2019 Overboard Ministries
All rights reserved.
ISBN-13: 978-1-943635-22-1

This book is also available as an eBook.
Visit www.overboardministries.com for details.

CONTENTS

FOREWORD

"How does it feel to kill?" That has been one of the most common questions I've been asked since my return from Vietnam. None of those who asked were being malicious or derogatory, just curious.

One of my editors, after sitting and talking to me, exclaimed, "You seem different than other Vietnam veterans I've talked to! You seem more grounded and less affected."

My response to both the question and comment was, "I had an awesome support system: God, the family he gave me, and his wonderful church I grew up in. I looked to God's word, followed his leading, and celebrated the prayer warriors who held me up before our Lord."

I know the weapons I directed at my targets caused death and destruction, but I was never present for an enemy's final breath nor have I wondered about them.

During the heat of battle, there is no time for those kinds of thoughts. My job was to protect and defend our troops on the ground. The military provided me with the tools to do the job; I used them and have never dwelled on the outcome. I was usually too busy with the next assignment.

The results of battles didn't make it to the pilots or our commanders until weeks, if not months, afterwards. I thank the Lord for his infinite mercy and love as he kept my mind free to do my best at the task he had called me to do.

During my Vietnam year, I often thought of David and his many battles, joys, and dangers. God pulled him through and blessed him greatly. I am not a king, but I have been protected and abundantly blessed.

"What about church? Did you have one?" a friend asked.

In Basic Training I went once. Unfortunately, there were no Bible-believing or preaching chaplains at Fort Polk, Fort Wolters, or Fort Rucker. I did manage to find services in nearby towns when allowed off base, and when on leave at my grandma's church.

In Vietnam I never saw a chaplain! The fact of the matter was, most of the time I had no idea what day it was. I had my Bible and read it regularly. My family sent church bulletins and Bible study books, but for the most part I was on my own to study as the Lord led.

It was not until I was married and assigned to Fort Wolters that we found a Bible-believing church that welcomed us into its membership.

My hope is that when you read my story, you will see God's awesome love and protection. He used me in ways I never could have imagined and showed me the power of prayer.

Don't ever forget God listens and answers his children's petitions, not always in the way they expect, but always for their best.

Acknowledgements

I want to thank professor Jim Hills of Corban University for guiding, directing, and editing me through this writing process. I have never received as many red correction marks on my writing as I did from Jim during this project. Thank you!

I could not have finished this book without my wife Peggy, and daughters Lisa and Stacy, who all pushed me onward through the finish.

Finally, thank you to the Overboard Ministries crew for all your hard work to make this book a reality!

CHAPTER ONE
NUMBERS

From the day of my birth, numbers have played an integral part in my life. Before my parents gave me a name or the government issued me a Social Security number, I was known as: Baby Eggerth, white male, 12/13/1945, 6:10 a.m., 7 pounds 9.5 ounces, 21.5 inches long.

As I've grown older, numbers have grown in meaning and significance. Romans 3:23 and John 3:16 became very important. They led me to a personal relationship with my Lord and Savior Jesus Christ.

The next series of numbers were related to education. Most children in my generation were not expected to attend any sort of preschool or kindergarten, but my parents paid to send me to private kindergarten at Bethel Christian Academy.

For a five-year-old to have to leave his happy home each morning, where he could play with and pester his younger brother, well, that was traumatic. Who cares that Dick and Jane run, or that one plus one equals two? I wanted my black and white TV, Flash Gordon, Cecil the Sea Serpent, and Howdy Doody.

I attended Bethel through 5th grade. Numbers were very good to me at that small, Christ-centered bastion of education. The enrollment was so small, the teachers could spend more time with each student. When I joined public school for 6th grade, the numbers showed I was two years above grade level.

I attended public school from 6th grade through high school. Math, Algebra, Geometry, Algebra II, and Calculus all became more and more difficult, and useful, as my knowledge expanded.

During my high school years, our country had become embroiled in a distant conflict: "Vietnam," they called it.

The situation in Vietnam was rapidly eating up the fuel needed to maintain its viability, namely manpower. The only solution to this problem was "The Draft."

In an attempt to make the process "fair," a system had been devised where all males, 18 to 25 years of age, were ordered to register with their local Selective Service office, also known as the Draft Board.

I was issued a computer-generated number based on my birth date. This number determined the order registered men were called into service. My number was 4 29 45 821. I still have no idea what those numbers stood for.

Several meaningful circumstances altered the call-up date for young potential draftees. Marriage, children, health issues (my brother Mike was exempt due to flat feet), and full-time college schedules were some of the many circumstances the Draft Board considered.

Western Baptist Bible College altered my call-up date. If I maintained a full college schedule, and kept my grades at a satisfactory level, my date would be put on hold.

Unfortunately, I had not turned in my English midterm paper. My teacher kept warning that not doing so could result in me failing the class.

I decided to drop the class instead of chancing failure, which would cause me to lose my place on the basketball team. I learned very soon it also caused me to lose my favorable draft status.

My "Draft Physical Notice" arrived in the mail a few days after dropping the class; the change had put me below the full-time student level.

My first experience with the military involved my draft physical. I was ordered to report for the physical on October 1, 1965, at 7:00 a.m.

My friend Dan also found himself in the same predicament. So there we were, standing in line in our underwear, answering questions, while being poked and prodded.

We were given a card that contained instructions as to which line we were to join for each medical test they needed to perform. The eye exam was simple and completed quickly.

The attending doctor pointed to the chart and instructed us to read what he was pointing at. The nurse would chart the doctor's findings, fill out the form, sign our card, and send us off to the next line.

It wasn't bad until we came to the line that led to a curtain. Once I reached the front of the line, a nurse led me behind the curtain and instructed me to pull my underwear down to my knees. I looked at her, then at the doctor, who was standing in front of me putting on a pair of rubber gloves. "Bend over, face the nurse, and spread your legs," he said.

Several humiliating hours later, they sent us home and told us to wait for the results.

Three days later, a postcard informed me I had passed my physical. It also contained my draft card; it showed I was 1-A, draft eligible. Dan's being the same, we decided to "beat the draft," and go talk to an Army recruiter.

Dan and I both loved working on cars and belonged to our church's car club, where we worked on my beautiful 1956 yellow and gold Chevrolet Bel Air. It seemed quite logical that two 19-year-olds who loved cars would make great Army mechanics.

If we were going to spend the next few years in the U.S. Army, we might as well be doing something we loved. Army grease is the same as civilian grease. The vehicles were larger but that only made them easier to work on.

Our draft orders had arrived within days of our draft cards. I was ordered to report for induction on December 13, 1965 – my 20th birthday, and Dan, a few days later.

The sergeant at the enlistment office was so nice; he even took our draft orders and tore them up. "Sign here and here and you're in the Army. Just need to take a few aptitude tests and you and your pal are off to mechanic's school." It sounded so easy!

Aptitude tests are a series of questions, developed by sociologists, to evaluate an individual's capabilities, strengths, and weaknesses.

"Does the applicant have a tendency to overreact?" "Will he be able to take orders and follow them faithfully?" "Does he have any special skills that could be of use during his military service?"

My test showed someone who was physically coordinated, not prone to panic, a problem solver, and had a tendency to stick it out through thick and thin. I had the aptitude to become a military helicopter pilot.

Dan's aptitude showed him to be "strong, confident, with good judgment," a candidate for MP school. That would be "military police" for you civilians.

The military uses aptitude tests as their Bible, no compromises, not even if promises were made – so much for mechanics school; besides, they needed pilots and MPs.

A week later, Dan shipped off to Basic Training at Fort Ord, California. He did his MP training at Fort Huachuca, Arizona.

I was subjected to more physical and academic testing, and finally to a board of three officers, two captains, and a major, who grilled me for several hours. They were acquainted with the extensive testing I'd undergone, and were intent on double checking those conclusions.

They quizzed me on my personal background: "Where were you born?" "What do you want to do when you leave the military?" Deductive reasoning brought questions like, "What would you do if you were driving on the freeway and a car came at you head on?" "If someone you didn't know asked you where you were going to be stationed and what you were going to do, would you be loyal to your country by answering or not answering?" It was very stressful!

I remember one of the captains, the only female board member, telling me I was too skinny to be able to fly a helicopter. I protested, flexed my bicep, and told her I was stronger than I looked. I was six feet tall and weighed 115 pounds at the time.

In spite of my "show of strength," they passed me onto Basic Training at Fort Polk, Louisiana.

At Fort Polk, my fellow recruits and I stepped off an old green Army bus, one of three. We had flown to Houston from California, and bussed from there.

After a short roll call, we were ushered to a large parking lot. It didn't have the usual parking stripes; instead, it was full of numbers. The numbers were in four groups of 30.

As our names were called, in alphabetical order, we were assigned one of those numbers. I was given number 14.

It was early afternoon when we arrived. We were given only one order: "Stay on your number."

Several sergeants came and gave us the once-over, sometimes talking to us, but more often than not giving us a disgusted look, turning on their heels, and leaving. We were a motley crew, some with long hair, some wearing shorts, most with a few too many pounds around the waist.

I remember standing for long periods of time, and then sitting on my travel bag, trying to get comfortable. It was hot and the asphalt gave off a strong oily smell.

Our attending sergeant occasionally broke the monotony with potty breaks and special assignments, such as "policing" the area around our numbers. We were lined up at one end of a large grass field, told to get on our hands and knees, and to pick up anything in front of us that wasn't green or moved. That was the cleanest, greenest, neatest field I have ever seen.

Gleefully, the sergeant lined up the first group of 30, my group, and marched us single file into a nearby building. There were several barber chairs in the center of the room. I remember the barber asking the recruit ahead of me if he wanted to save his sideburns; he said "yes," so the barber had him cup his hands under his ears and shaved the remnants into his palms.

As we left the building, the sergeant inspected his new "bald" recruits with a smile of satisfaction. So much for individuality!

Around 5:00 p.m., we were lined up and marched to the "chow hall" (that would be military for lunch room). It smelled wonderful! As I moved along the line, I saw foods similar to what I normally ate: mashed potatoes, green beans, corn, and okra. It was not until I reached the main course that I stopped in my tracks.

I have always loved pork, but as I peered through the sneeze guard and saw a large hunk of pork roast floating in a sea of orange grease, my stomach did a flip.

I kept my composure, took the unsightly pork, and moved on to better things – dessert! There it was a beautiful piece of apple pie.

My friends and I found an empty table and ate our first military meal. It actually tasted better than it looked and I could hardly wait for that apple pie. But when I finally plunged into my dessert and lifted my fork for the first bite, I was shocked when the only taste my brain registered was "pineapple!" Don't get me wrong, pineapple makes a great upside-down cake. I can even enjoy a nice piece of pineapple pie…if I know what it is.

But my taste buds had been prepared for apple pie; my mind could not wrap itself around this great disappointment. So much for my first military meal!

Now it was back to our numbers and the finish of our first day of military service. There was more sitting, standing, policing the area, and just being bored, but at least the sergeant was there to keep us busy. I wondered what breakfast would be like.

Northwest Louisiana has an average temperature of 64 degrees in the daytime, 41 at night, and 70 percent humidity during February. With the sun rapidly setting, we became anxious about where we would sleep. I just couldn't picture myself curled up on this nice, soft asphalt with 30 very aromatic young men!

I was not totally unfamiliar with Northern Louisiana; after all, my grandparents lived only 150 miles to the north. I spent most every summer hunting, fishing, camping, and swimming in and around the bayous.

I knew the terrain, the swamps, and local flora and fauna. There are plenty of rattle snakes, water moccasins, alligators, ticks, and redbugs.

My cousins and I would use my uncle's flat-bottom boat to fish the cypress-lined swamp, known to us as "The Bodcau."

Uncle Jamie always left his boat upside down on the shore, paddles hidden in the bushes. His instructions were to always hit the bottom of the boat with a paddle; this cleared snakes out of their nice cool hiding places under the seats.

We fished for bluegill, crappie, small-mouth bass, and gigged for frogs. Frog gigging had its ups and downs; we left the house just as the sun was setting, dressed in shorts and tennis shoes, no socks. Gigging gear consisted of a flash light, a canvas bag, and a frog gig.

A frog gig is a three-pronged, hooked trident on the end of a broom stick. We attempted to stab the gig into the frog and then slip them into the bag.

We would wade into the Bodcau, the smell of cypress in our nostrils, green ooze squishing between our toes, and listen for frogs. We would push pass the snakes and alligator gar, all in an attempt to fill our canvas bags with fat, delicious frogs.

Redbugs, also known as chiggers, or "no see ums," as the local Indians called them, are everywhere. Walk across the grass, they're there on your ankles, brush against a bush, and they're on your arms.

These bugs are clear, almost see-through, when they first attach themselves. When they start feeding, they turn blood red, thus the name redbug. The itch they cause is awful. They love the warmest places on your body, any place with hair.

6

These were the things going through my mind as I laid my head on my soft-sided travel bag staring into the growing dusk. I was not used to sleeping on asphalt. We were all holding out hope that a nice, soft bed was still in our near future.

As the light faded and darkness set in, our hope ended. We were destined to spend the remainder of this night on our numbers. Good old number 14 for me!

One would think the United States Army would provide blankets, but our military numbers still hadn't been attached, so we were in that limbo state of non-existence.

I was dressed in Levi's, a short-sleeve shirt, white Converse high-top tennis shoes. No jacket.

My small bag contained socks, underwear, and toiletries. No soft mattress or extra padding to be found there. It was destined to be a long evening.

The sun set behind the white oak trees. In the fading light, the stars appeared on the dark blanket that was night. It might have been beautiful except for the annoying flood lights that shone down from the side of the nearby building.

Maybe they kept the lights on because they were afraid we might change our minds and run away. Not me! I knew what was out there in the dark, humid, and noisy night.

Time moves very slowly when you're trying to sleep in a new and unknown place on an asphalt mattress and no comfy pillow.

At about 1:00 or 2:00 a.m., the very long day started to numb our senses. I laid my head on my bag and dozed until 4:00 a.m.

Lying there, looking up at the starry night sky, and then at my watch, the hours between 4:00 and 6:00 a.m. passed like molasses from a cold glass jar.

It was cooler during the night, but Louisiana is always humid. One summer, I remember my wife asking my cousin if she should bring a sweater since it might cool off after dark; my cousin's response was a hearty series of knowing laughs. It never cools much and it's always humid.

Darkness was fading; I could discern the outline of the oak trees. If I close my eyes….

Dawn broke to find everyone covered in morning dew. We were stiff and sore as we woke from our restless sleep.

Sarge, drinking his hot cup of morning coffee, got us up and started our day with calisthenics, a few jumping jacks, lots of pushups and stretches, followed by policing the area. I was so tired I do not remember marching to, or even eating, breakfast.

Sometime during the mid-morning hours, our company sergeants showed up and marched us to the quartermaster.
All military clothes and supplies are issued by the supply sergeant who works for the quartermaster.

Arms extended, I was issued three pairs of green fatigue pants, three green fatigue shirts, a sleeve of olive drab boot socks, a set of olive drab undershirts, underwear, and one olive drab ball cap.

At the next station I received a universal fatigue jacket and two pairs of black Army boots. Further down the line, a young private took my papers and printed four tags with my last name and stitched them to my shirts and jacket.

When I arrived at the final station, I received two dog tags containing my full name, rank, serial number, religion, and blood type. They had us look carefully at our tags. If we were on the battlefield and in need of a blood transfusion, they'd look at our dog tags and pump in what it says. If you are type A and your tag shows B, you could be in real trouble.

The numbers had finally added up. I had received my U.S. Army serial number.

One thing we noticed very quickly – an enlisted man's serial number started with R.A. for "Regular Army." But the guys who were drafted had U.S. "Conscripted" in front of their number.

It didn't mean much yet to Basic trainees, but it did mean something to our trainers. The sergeants remembered who was a U.S. and who was an R.A. They were tough on R.A.'s but they were much tougher on U.S.'s.

They took it personally that someone had to be drafted into their beloved Army. If there was a nasty duty—cleaning toilets, digging ditches, or shoveling snow—they would find a draftee or two to do the dirty work.

My number was attached to every paper the Army issued on me; it was indelibly etched in my mind through verbal repetition.

With a sergeant planted in my face demanding my serial number, it soon became an extension of my identity. I'm so glad I was R.A.! The U.S.'s lingered much longer under the sergeant's intense glare.

The first piece of paper, or order, was to assign me to my new unit. I was now officially Eggerth, RA19874609, PVT, Delta Company,

4th Battalion, 1st Training Brigade, Fort Polk, Louisiana. It was February 14, 1966.

I had finally arrived; I was a real United States Army private.

CHAPTER TWO
D-4-1

With arms full of new Army gear, we marched, dog tags clinking, into our home for the next three months.

The smell of old wood and floor wax filled our nostrils as we filed into the first floor, building one, of Delta Company.

The sergeants assigned us a bed, each with sheets and blankets folded neatly at the foot, and then proceeded to teach us the "Army way" of making them. We were also taught the finer points of storing our new Army gear in our Army-issue footlockers.

All the beds in the barracks were bunks. My new bunkmate, Mark, was much larger than I, so I took the top bunk.

Mark had a few "minor" problems that became more and more evident as training commenced. He was headed for the infantry, so most of his problems were within Army specs.

For example, marching was not his forte. He didn't actually have two left feet, but it took him lots of practice to get his feet to stay in rhythm with the sergeants' sing-song cadence. The most frustrating of his problems occurred in the early hours of each training day; Mark could not make a bed. As hard as he tried, it never met the sergeants' exacting standards.

Every morning a sergeant would go from bunk to bunk and bounce a quarter off each newly-made bed. If the quarter bounced, we moved onto our next assigned tasks – sweep the floor, dust the shelves, or the U.S.'s main task, to clean the latrine (bathroom, for you civilians). If our bed did not bounce the quarter, he would grab the mattress and dump it on the floor. This circus would continue until our bed met his tyrannical satisfaction.

The sergeant became more and more frustrated with Mark's bed making, until finally, looking at me, he said, "Help him get his bed made, NOW!" It was several frustrating, irritating, aggravating weeks until he became proficient enough to get the quarter to bounce.

Don't think I didn't have my own bed-making problems. Having your bed dumped, sheets dragging dust from the floor, is a great incentive to get it right!

Mark was from the Ozarks and what he lacked in social and physical skills, he made up for with his rifle. He was the most accurate marksman in our unit. Day after day, he knocked the center of the target into oblivion. He easily qualified "expert." I was an average marksman.

I enjoyed my friendship with Mark; he was a kind and gentle human being. He told me when he left the military he wanted to start his own hunting guide business. I hope it worked out for him.

One of our first duty assignments was "fireguard." All of Fort Polk's barracks are wooden. These buildings have been around since World War II and as they aged, they became drier, more brittle, and susceptible to fire. It would not have been so dangerous if it wasn't for the fact that they were still heated with wood-burning stoves.

Every member of the platoon would take many turns as fireguard.

Our loud, combat-experienced, Korean War veteran sergeants instructed us in the finer points and responsibilities of fireguard, and we gave them our undivided attention. The verbal threat of court martial, section eight, or a firing squad didn't hurt either.

There were two floors to each barracks, one platoon, and one fireguard for each floor. 1st Platoon was on the bottom floor, 2nd Platoon on the top.

Each guard would walk a one-hour shift, back and forth, round and round the barracks. He would check the doors and windows, and ensure the fire stayed in the stove. He was also responsible to make sure no one entered or left the barracks without the permission of the sleeping, on-duty sergeant.

There's a real play-on-words ("sleeping" and "on-duty"). The sergeants had a room in our barracks that the on-duty slept in so he would be readily available in case of emergency.

The smell of the oak logs snapping and crackling during the night gave the barracks a cozy, warm, homey feel.

This was our first lesson in military team building, guard duty, and personal responsibility.

Each evening, as the sun set, the sergeant produced the night-duty roster. When my name was on the list, it included a one-hour time period when I would be personally responsible for the well being of my platoon and the barracks proper.

It did not end there; the first soldier on duty was responsible to wake the next on the list, so on and so on, through the long, tiresome night. Another sergeant could, and often did, pop in at any time during the night.

On one occasion, the sergeant found no one on duty! Within seconds everyone in the barracks was standing at attention at the end of our bunks. The duty roster was pulled, each guard was grilled, and the last one to fulfill his duty was discovered. The guard had attempted to wake the next on the list, who had sat up, but never got out of bed. The on-duty guard had gone back to bed without ensuring his replacement was up and moving.

Both parties were subjected to hours of cleaning toilets with toothbrushes.

The platoon, still standing at the end of our bunks, was informed, face to face, what could happen if this ever happened again. The penalty for negligence, on duty, could be court martial. If negligence happened during war and someone died, it could mean jail, or even the firing squad.

Once, the guard I tried to wake jumped up and yelled, "On guard!" We had just finished three intense days of hand-to-hand combat. Waking a sleeping soldier can be quite dangerous, even if he didn't have his gun. He finally got out of bed and assumed his duty, and I went back to bed.

My only other experience with guard duty came one windy, damp evening when the duty truck picked us up in front of our barracks. One other soldier and I were assigned to guard the golf course club house. Rifles in hand, no bullets, we walked back and forth the next two hours. We were to stay in close contact, never out of each other's sight, challenging anyone with, "Halt, who goes there?" "Advance and be recognized!" "What's the password?"

Fortunately, we never had to utter those words. No one came anywhere near our duty station that night.

I'm not saying we didn't have some exciting moments. On one occasion we heard sounds of movement just outside our vision. We both stood quiet, listening for the next sound. Just about that time, a scrawny cow, chewing its cud, stepped into the moonlight. Oh! Well, so much for protecting Fort Polk from potential alien life forms.

It took several days, but we finally had our barracks in top military shape. Our uniforms were pressed and boots polished. The sergeants were so impressed that the next morning, at 2:00 a.m., they came bursting through the door, turned on the lights, and ordered us to the end of our bunks. We were told to put on our boots and assemble on the street, in the rain.

I don't remember what was running through my head at the time, but I do remember what my firstborn son, Todd, had to say when his mom woke him for his second day of school. He was five at the time. He looked out the rain-soaked window, turned, and went back to bed. His mom came in a few minutes later and said, "Get up or you'll be late for school!" His response was, "You mean I have to go in the rain?"

There we were, 30 young men, in platoon formation, standing at attention, in boots, underwear, and rain ponchos. We were marched to the dirt track and, still in platoon formation, jogged and ran, jogged and ran, for an hour. My legs felt like rubber. Back in our barracks, we fell exhausted into our bunks. I'm sure glad I didn't have fire guard that night.

At 5:00 a.m., after "Reveille," we were back out of our bunks, making our beds and getting dressed in olive drab t-shirts, fatigue pants, boots, and no ponchos. The rain had stopped.

We assembled in front of the barracks and marched to the parade grounds for morning calisthenics: jumping jacks, pushups, crunches, stretches, and running. Having gotten our blood flowing, the sergeants marched us to the chow hall for a well-earned hot breakfast. Those Army pancakes tasted as good as mom's!

Returning to our barracks, we put on our uniform shirts and marched off to our morning classes. Army classes for Basic Training consisted of our sergeants lecturing and demonstrating skills we were to practice most of the afternoon: hand-to-hand combat, care and use of rifles, hand grenades, bayonets, and gas masks.

Several weeks into training, we were placed at the end of our bunks and called one at a time to the rifle rack. The chained-and-locked rack ran down the middle of the barracks floor.

As a sergeant called our name, a second sergeant would remove a rifle and read the number engraved on the metal core. He would then hand it to the named soldier if the numbers on the list and rifles matched.

That rifle, now attached to us through Army paperwork, would rapidly become an extension of our bodies.

Training with that new extension began almost immediately. We had to learn how to carry the weapon while marching, running, exercising, and parading.

The shooting range would come later. First, we had to learn to take it apart and put it back together, blindfolded. The smell of gun oil soon permeated our skin and clothes.

Each morning, the armament soldier, a member of our platoon, would unlock the rifle rack with the key hung by chain around his neck, and hand out the assigned weapons. The routine was reversed before and after meals, and then again at bed time. Sleeping and eating were the only times the weapon didn't fully occupy our every waking moment.

We had our weapons at our sides as we did morning calisthenics. The Army had a way of including new equipment into everyday activities. We would lie on our backs and use the rifle as weights, or cradle the rifle in our arms and crawl. The Army can be creative. Doing sit-ups with a rifle held against your chest built character as well as muscle.

It was bad enough running in boots, but now we had to carry a 12-pound rifle and sling. The Army is a professional at pain.

On one of our nightly visits to the exercise track, rifles held out in front of us, my friend Larry was jogging along on the outside edge of our formation. About the third time around the quarter-mile dirt track, his boot caught on a tree root, causing him to fall forward. Most of us near him heard a loud "crack." The formation continued forward.

It wasn't until later we learned Larry had fallen on his rifle and the cracking sound was the rifle stock breaking in half. Larry was 230 pounds of solid muscle. I weighed in at a solid 125. I'm glad it wasn't me; the sound probably would have been my arm. It was not only exhausting, but often dangerous to be a U.S. Army private, even in training.

Our company commander, Captain G., was a no-nonsense career officer. He left the training to his team, but loved marching, and was always ready to lead us on a long, sweaty, mile burner. We had packs, rifle, and heavy boots; he had comfy fatigues and walking boots.

I learned a new and valuable skill during these early marches – sleeping while standing. We were given five-minute breaks as the sergeant saw fit. He would stop the column and say, "Smoke them if you have them!" Those of us who did not have such a habit took the opportunity to catch a nice short "nap."

Most civilians might ask, "How could you go to sleep so fast?" My response would be, "Five hours, or less, sleep each night and lots of exercise makes napping easy, no matter who you are."

Our executive officer, on the other hand, was a young lieutenant who loved to mess with us. On one occasion, after a few days of rain, he called the platoon out for a short march.

With a sergeant trailing behind, Lieutenant D. marched the entire platoon through the largest mud hole he could find. He called the platoon to a halt right in the middle of the mud.

It was late in the evening. The sergeant was not happy about the platoon being pulled from its normal routine, and Lieutenant D. had us standing in mud.

All in all, things were not totally out of the ordinary until the lieutenant yelled, "I will be back at 6:00 a.m., and this platoon had better be in top military shape." Lieutenant D. then walked off and left us standing in the mud. The sergeant marched us back to our barracks, told us to clean our boots, and retired to his office.

Half an hour later, the other three sergeants came storming through the front door. After putting their heads together, each sergeant grabbed a squad and began making the barracks shine.

Around 2:00 in the morning, we were sitting on our lockers polishing both pairs of boots. The dry pair went smoothly but the wet pair took several layers of boot polish before they passed the sergeant's trained eye.

Because we were working all night, we stripped our beds and hung our blankets over the windows to avoid the attention of the night patrols and duty officer. We didn't want to be caught with the barracks lights on after "Taps," the bugle call for lights out. The sergeants would have to justify their decision to have the platoon's lights on, Captain G. would have to make a full report to the general's office, and the lieutenant could be in deep trouble.

At 10 minutes to 6:00, the platoon was ready. Our beds were made, boots polished, and the barracks was shining. We were standing at attention at the foot of our bunks when the clock struck 6:00. Then it was 6:15, then 6:30, but still no Lieutenant D. At 6:45 the lead sergeant stormed into his office and called Captain G. He showed up a short time later. He earned a great deal of respect as he inspected the barracks and each soldier as we stood at attention at the foot of our beds. Captain G. was a man of honor, a gentleman, and a true asset to the United States Army.

We heard later there was a very heated discussion in the captain's office between the captain and his first officer.

One Saturday evening, just before lights out, the sergeant had the armament soldier counting the secured rifles. We were one rifle short. We had checked our rifles out for cleaning earlier that day but had secured them prior to lunch.

The sergeant checked each rifle until the missing rifle was matched to the soldier to whom it was assigned. The private pleaded that he had checked in the rifle and had no idea where it could be. The sergeant grabbed his mattress and threw it to the floor; it was not hidden among the sheets, or under his mattress.

The entire platoon was sent to check every bed, closet, locker, nook, and cranny. There was still no rifle!

Entering the office, the sergeant called his team, and finally Captain G. Within the hour, the entire company command team was present, except Lieutenant D., who could not be found. He was single so that was not unusual.

The four sergeants and our captain repeated the procedure that had been followed earlier. All bunks were stripped of mattresses; every inch of the barracks was searched by one or more of the command team, including an intense search of the outside area. Still no rifle.

You do not lose your rifle, not in combat, not in training. The paperwork goes clear to the Pentagon.

Because Lieutenant D. had not checked in, Captain G. decided to suspend the search until morning, when the military police would have to be notified.

Early the next morning, Lieutenant D. checked in. He had removed the rifle while we were at lunch. He and some friends had gone shooting at the rifle range, and then out to dinner, and they hadn't finished until it was too late to return the rifle, he said.

Captain G. was not happy when he called Lieutenant D. to his office that Sunday morning.

The soldier assigned the weapon and the armament soldier had been in the hot seat. Both soldiers could have been court-martialed, as well as having to pay the Army for the missing equipment.

During World War II, bills were issued for missing tanks, planes, and even an occasional ship. Most items were found or proven to be destroyed or sunk, which relieved the assigned individual of responsibility.

Lieutenant D. was a young, inexperienced officer who had not yet realized his place in the vast expanse known as the U.S Army.

As I recall, there were no further incidents involving young Lieutenant D.

Rifles and pugil sticks don't seem to have much in common. A pugil stick looks like a giant Q-tip; it's a six-foot-long, 1½-inch-thick oak pole with padding on each end, and weighs around 20 pounds.

Not wanting to lose or damage its newly obtained recruits, the Army substitutes the pugil stick for the rifle during hand-to-hand combat training.

"Thrusts" and "parries" are moves done with your rifle in close-quarters combat. A thrust pushes the muzzle and bayonet into your enemy's solar plexus. A parry uses the rifle to push away your enemy's weapon when he attacks you. It didn't feel good being hit with a pugil stick. I can't imagine being hit with an unpadded rifle.

During practice, the sergeants would pair trainees according to size and weight. We wore padded helmets and hand and crotch guards during contact.

The first time we did actual contact, we were in two lines, facing each other. We were given the order, "Fight!" After a few swings, with very little contact, our disgusted sergeant grabbed my stick; he had been standing behind me, and put me at attention. He looked at my opponent and said, "Hit him!"

Now I cannot be sure what was going through my mind at that moment, but I can assure you I was not looking forward to what was about to occur.

My adversary looked at me and then at the sergeant who said, "Hit him NOW!" He swung and hit me in the side of the helmet. I must say I have been hit harder during football games and with an occasional baseball, but it still stung.

The sergeant was not impressed! He snatched the stick from his hand and said, "When I say hit him, I mean HIT him," and took a powerful swing at my opponent, sending him flipping backwards to the ground.

There was stunned silence as the platoon watched our fellow member attempt to rise from the dirt.

The silence was broken when the sergeant thrust the stick back into my chest and said, "HIT HIM!" I looked at the stick, the sergeant, and then at my opponent, who had finally returned to the formation.

There are certain things that occur naturally that ensure human survival: heart beats, breathing, and running from bears are some examples. Apparently my mind had accepted this was one of "those things."

I turned my attention to my opponent, who was attempting to shake off the effects of the sergeant's recent "demonstration." He was

Pugil stick practice

swaying back and forth and did not look to be mentally present.

Without another thought, I reared back and unloaded my best shot to the side of his helmet.

I have often wondered if he was even aware he was back in the dirt a second time.

What happened next was military basic training. The sergeant yelled at the top of his voice, "Everyone fights NOW."

With the same survival instinct, the entire platoon began an epic battle matched only by a few historic events, e.g., "Custer's Last Stand," "The Alamo," and maybe "Joshua's Battle at Jericho."

It seemed like hours, but actually minutes, that we battled until the sergeant was fully satisfied with the carnage.

Any female reading this might not understand how such an event could occur in our seemingly modern civilization. Let me just say, "Testosterone!" It is against the male ego to allow him to be bested, especially by one of equal size, weight, and training.

However, in this case, when the Sarge said "STOP," the entire platoon wilted, like a bunch of water-starved flowers, in utter exhaustion.

Under normal circumstances, a male does not forget being bested, or tied. In this case, we were just happy to have survived. It actually built a solid camaraderie that never faded.

No one talked about what happened. We had been challenged and the entire platoon had met that challenge. The sergeants were satisfied; we were ready! Our military careers were in full swing.

There are a few other events that my memory still sees clearly, even after 50 plus years.

Rifle qualifications

I was so intent on hitting the targets, I didn't realize there was blood dripping down my chin. My right thumbnail had gouged deep into the corner of my lip during the rifle's recoil, and blood was flowing down my cheek and hand. It painted the corner of my green fatigue shirt crimson.

I qualified Sharpshooter! My lip was sore and swollen but life was good.

Grenades

We spent a week talking about, and throwing, five-pound practice grenades. We learned the kill radius, injury probabilities, and how to disarm a defective grenade.

I was BAD at tossing grenades, really BAD! I couldn't throw those metal pineapples far enough to ensure my own safety. Following my first and only throw of a live grenade, the sergeant jumped on top of me. He later said he had to save my life.

There was a concrete bunker in front of me, so I'm sure it was punishment for ineptitude, rather than safety.

NEVER VOLUNTEER

The last real character-building event occurred on our final field training march. This was a 16-mile forced march in full pack, with rifle.

I heard they were looking for a "guidon bearer." This soldier carried a 13-pound oak pole with the company's insignia attached to the top.

I began to think, hmm, a 13-pound stick versus a 30-pound pack and 16-pound rifle. This seemed to be a no-brainer! I piped up, "I'll carry the guidon!" You know, company pride and all that...

My dad, as well as several ex-military men from church had told me again and again, "Don't volunteer for anything, ever; it can only lead to trouble."

I went to collect the guidon and asked the Sarge what to do with my pack, which now contained half of a two-man tent, rolled above the pack, another six pounds.

With a smile he said, "You carry it!"

"Oh!" "Well!" "Really?"

"Yes!" he replied. "Get the pole and get out front. We're ready to go!"

The military won't let you unvolunteer. I was stuck!

The captain, decked out in his crisply-ironed fatigues, lightweight training helmet, and soft, comfortable boots, motioned me to the front of the column. His instructions were, "Be on the right side of the column opposite me."

Not long after we started, he exclaimed, "Stay one step behind me and keep up!"

All four platoons, ours leading the formation, started off at a brisk pace. We were a handsome group, stepping proudly out, flag waving, heading for our assigned bivouac. Only 16 miles to go!

Every few miles, the captain would call a halt and allow us to catch our breath and rotate our platoons. 1st Platoon would drop back to the rear of the column and 2nd Platoon moved forward. This continued until each platoon had been in the lead.

When we left the company area, the formation was tight. The sergeants kept their respective platoons moving smoothly.

But I noticed that as the mile marks started to move farther apart as we advanced, the proud formation started to look ragtag.

I, on the other hand, remained in my position. There was no relief! My fatigue grew with the miles as they fell away behind us.

It wasn't much later the captain glanced over at me and yelled, "You're slowing down, Eggerth. Pick it up!" He was using me to decide when to take our next break, and its length.

A little over three-quarters of the way to our destination, he looked at me and said, "See that marker over there? That's where the last guidon bearer collapsed. I bet you won't last much longer!"

I do not remember my response, if any, but I decided I was not going to quit. They would have to forcibly remove this pole from my cold, dead hands.

It was a great mercy when the captain told me to turn right into a large open area and plant the flag. We had made it! Our platoon sergeant motioned me to a nearby area and said, "1st Platoon will tent up here. Wait here till they all arrive."

Our platoon had regained the lead position, but was stretched out over a long distance. Just a few of the hardiest had stayed up with the captain.

I remember flopping on the ground and releasing my pack. The next thing I remember, the Sarge was pairing us off and having us put up our tents. My friend Rob helped me up, and we put our tent halves together and prepared for the night.

It was well over an hour before the last of the company arrived, many of them in or on a field ambulance. Several actually were admitted to the hospital.

There were consequences to my ill-advised volunteering. I lost feeling in both sets of toes. Most returned within several months, but some feeling has never returned.

Our very last march was for the graduation parade. We again formed in front of our barracks, marched to the parade grounds, and joined the rest of our training battalion for graduation.

Alpha company led the way, followed by Bravo, Charlie, Delta (our company), and finally Echo.

After the company finished the pass by, we formed the battalion facing the general. It was a warm day and we had been told not to lock our knees, lest we pass out from the heat.

The general was in full graduation form and droned on for what seemed an hour. At least a dozen of our platoon crashed to the ground during the ceremony and lay there until it was over. I wonder if they all really did faint!

I was one of two promoted to Private First Class, at the captain's request, at the end of Basic. Volunteering and keeping up with him wasn't the brightest thing I'd ever done, but it showed him tenacity and some leadership skills. This made me feel good, but we were all promoted to sergeant upon arriving at flight school. Finally, but most importantly, I came to realize I could do more than I ever believed I was capable of.

Practically everyone in our platoon had been pulled for K.P. (kitchen patrol). But I had escaped! No K.P. for me. Yahoo!

We were preparing to go on leave and then flight school, when Sarge came into the barracks with some bad news: "You men headed for flight school have been put on hold for 10 days. You will be staying here until your orders come through."

Oh well! We'll have 10 days to relax before leave and flight school, I thought.

Not so fast, private! The U.S. Army does not have slackers, so that meant 10 days of K.P. in the main post kitchen.

Every morning at 5:00 a.m., we marched to the kitchen, aided the cooks preparing breakfast, and washed dishes, pots, and pans. This was repeated at lunch! We finally marched back to the barracks around 3:00 p.m.

My lunch assignment was in the potato-peeling room. There were two of us. One ran the potato peeler while the other lifted the 40-pound bags of raw potatoes and poured them into the machine.

The mess sergeant instructed us on the proper use of the machine, and warned us that it only took 10 seconds to peel 40 pounds – any longer and he would not be happy!

He put my partner on the platform above the machine, where the controls were. I was on the cold, wet, concrete floor, lifting bags of potatoes.

The smell of potatoes added an earthiness to the job.

The potatoes were kept in a dry room, just off our peeling room. My job was to carry the bags into the peeling room, fill the peeler, empty the peeler, clean the peeler, and keep the floor clean. Within the first 10 minutes, I was covered from head to foot in potato dirt and mud.

My partner pushed the button on and pushed the button off. Initially he remembered to keep track of the peeling time. But around the 3rd peeling, I filled the machine, and he closed and fastened the lid and turned it on.

This time though, he turned around and picked up a magazine that was sitting on his stool, and sat down. Moments later he jumped to his feet and pushed the control button off.

He lifted the lid, and we both peered into the peeler. Just then the mess sergeant strode into the peeler room. He jumped onto the control platform and also peered into the peeler.

His face turned several shades of red. I also believe there were clouds of steam streaming from each ear. He was having trouble regaining his composure and there was a mumbling sound coming from his mouth. Moments later he exploded in a flurry of profanity!

His precious potatoes were now the size of marbles. Well, the largest ones were. The smaller potatoes were now a thick, dirty soup running down the drain.

The sergeant was standing face to face with my partner, questioning his I.Q. and his right to be breathing this precious Army air. I almost felt sorry for him!

After the Sarge cooled down, he looked at me and said, "Get up here." I had left the stand when the sergeant's face turned more purple, then red. He gave me the same lecture he had given my partner and put me to work on the button. I became a real expert on 10-second timing.

I still had to do pots and pans, but anytime the mess sergeant needed potatoes, I was his man.

10 days later we said good bye to Fort Polk, Louisiana, and hello to flight school, Fort Wolters, Texas.

It was April, 19, 1966.

CHAPTER THREE
THE PROCESS OF WEEDING

I love popcorn. It has very little nutritional value, and even less when it's covered in butter and loaded with salt, but I love it! My dear friend Pastor Hills is the only person I've ever met who loves it more than I do. Any left from his evening snack would be eaten in a bowl for breakfast, with milk. I've never tried it, but he says it's delicious.

My little brother and I would be sitting on the sofa watching TV, when we'd hear the rattle of the iron skillet on our old gas range. Mom was making popcorn!

The "Pop! Pop! Pop!" of the corn caused our mouths to salivate. Then the aroma of the popping corn and melted butter would reach our nostrils.

Flash Gordon's dilemmas would be lost in the ecstasy of that wonderful smell and taste of popcorn!

One day, when I was seven or eight, I went to the hardware store with my dad. I became fascinated with the turning rack near the front counter that contained a variety of garden seeds. The packets pictured the produce that could be grown from the seeds inside.

I couldn't believe my eyes – POPCORN! You could grow popcorn! I pulled out a packet and approached my dad in nervous anticipation. "Can I please grow some popcorn?"

My dad looked at me and then at the package. Nervously I awaited his reply.

He smiled, I smiled, the man at the counter smiled. Dad pulled a nickel from his pocket and I became a popcorn farmer.

At the front curb of our property was a strip of dirt about five-feet wide and 20-feet long, to where our property ended.

My plan was to grow my crop in that vast acreage.

At seven years of age, I couldn't break the ground, but my dad could, and did. He explained all that was required, and supervised as I carried out my farming chores.

I gently buried each kernel, just as I was instructed. I watered, then waited. I guess that's what God has done through the ages. He planted his word in my heart as soon as I was old enough to listen. He started the "weeding process" in my life, and he has continued to this day.

Each morning I would go out and check my crop. It seemed like years, but finally one morning a small green shoot pushed its way through the dark earth. I was a farmer!

One by one, each seed burst from the ground in a glorious display of green. Neither the black asphalt of the street nor the locomotives on the tracks 100 feet away could discourage them or me.

What was that? That's not a corn plant! What is it?

I ran to find my dad. He looked closely at the new green invader and informed me, "It's a weed!"

"What do I do?" I asked.

"You get rid of it. It will choke your corn and steal its nourishment," he replied. He reached down and gently pulled the invader from the ground. "You must get it out before the roots run deep and tangle with the corn."

Each day I surveyed my crop and, following my father's example, I practiced the "weeding process." Eventually, I actually harvested the crop, and popped the dried seeds. Delicious!

I was about to be introduced to the Army's version of weeding, at Fort Wolters, Mineral Wells, Texas, starting May of 1966.

East Texas is flat. The ground rolls and swells like a calm day on the Pacific Ocean. There are no high hills or mountains to climb, nothing to give you elevation for a wide view. Scrub brush and cacti are scattered through out the region.

The Brazos River runs its zigzagging course west of the city. Some places it digs deep into the rolling Texas soil and forms shallow cliffs. Most places it's a slow-moving, sandy-bottom stream.

Mineral Wells rolls up its sidewalks at 6:00 p.m. every evening, except Friday and Saturday when the diners and bowling alley stay open till 10. Into this mellow, low-key atmosphere, the U.S. Army built Fort Wolters.

Our first few weeks at Wolters were devoted to officer training.

Brazos River

West Point and Officer Candidate School (O.C.S.) are dedicated to training young potential commissioned officers. Fort Wolters is dedicated to training helicopter pilots. Officer training is secondary; warrant officers do not, normally, command troops, so the training is not as specific. We needed to know how to be officers, but our responsibility was not as great.

We were used to saluting everyone. Soon we would have to return salutes, walk in the correct spot, with other officers, and be able to give orders as well as take them.

After getting our living unit and bed assignments, we met our commanding officer and his cadre. They would not be doing flight training; however, they did pre-flight classes and officer training.

Weeding the crop, that was their job. For some reason the Army did not want to trust its million-dollar helicopters to someone who could not function under pressure.

The pressure began immediately! The sergeants roared into our billet, got into our face, and started making us do pushups. Any mistakes brought physical and mental pressure.

At 12:01 p.m., if you accidentally said, "Good morning, sir," you and everyone on your floor did 25 pushups for not saying "good afternoon." You also did 25 more for daring to call a sergeant "sir." You never, ever, call a sergeant "sir." In their words, "You call me Sarge or Sergeant. I work for a living!"

This went on and on into the night. More and more pressure, more and more pushups. By morning, my arms and legs were aching. One candidate started crying. They took him away and we never saw him again.

Over the next two weeks, there was a steady trickle leaving the training unit. This flow was not sufficient for our "weeders."

To practice our future duties as officers, we were given command of the unit. One candidate was chosen as company commander and four for platoon leaders, one for each of the four platoons.

These duties usually lasted no longer than a few days. If we fulfilled the duties to the sergeant's satisfaction, we passed and never had that pressure again. If we messed up, they doubled the pressure; we either cracked, or corrected our mistakes.

My turn was coming soon.

We marched everywhere, so I decided to take a chance that would get me passed quickly, or send me packing.

Every day we were marched down the street, stopped, single filed into a parking lot, and then into class. When I became platoon leader, I decided instead of stopping, I would do a flanking move. Flanking means changing directions as a group, while moving. Left flank, you spin to the left. Right flank, you spin to the right.

We were moving down the street, the parking lot was on our right. I yelled, "Platoon, tighten up!"

We had been together as a group long enough to have built good camaraderie. The platoon's ears perked up and the sergeant quickly moved next to me.

In a loud clear voice, I yelled, "Right flank, march!" In perfect unison they spun right and moved into the parking lot. Two steps from the grass, I yelled, "Platoon, halt!" My dear, wonderful friends stopped inches from the grass.

The sergeant ran to the edge of the grass, stomped back and forth, came over, got in my face, and said, "It's a good thing no one stepped on my grass!" I had been on the spot, as platoon leader, for only 20 minutes. When we got out of class, I was back in the platoon. Whew! Thank you, Lord!

The pressure on the platoon continued! Not only were we dealing with the sergeants, but the flight class that was about to graduate was also assigned to aid them in their torture campaign against us.

On one occasion, my five roommates and I were in our room cleaning, when someone, looking out our second-story window, saw a group of our adversaries coming into the barracks.

One of my roommates made a comment about being tired of doing pushups. We looked at each other and decided to hide. We climbed out the window, dangled our feet over the ledge, and waited.

The commotion inside the building rose to a loud din. We heard someone enter our room, but he left when no one appeared to be home. The platoon must have done at least 100 pushups, while we relaxed outside in the shade.

Days later, it got deathly quiet around our barracks. No one came to pressure us – no marching and no pushups. Pre-flight and officer training were over! It was time to learn to fly!

Now that we had survived early "weeding," they knew we were going to need flight equipment. The sergeants marched us back to the quartermaster's, but this time we were going after something special – our flight suits and flight helmets.

Flight suits are unique to aviation. They are a nylon and cotton mix, lightweight, long sleeved, with pockets for everything. Pencils and pens are nestled on our left shoulder. Small zippered pockets hold aviator sunglasses and other valuables. Large zippered leg pockets hold maps. Pockets for everything an aviator might need for expected or unexpected events.

Helmets are even more specific for aviation. They are equipped with pull-down visors, one made of clear plastic to protect eyes from flying objects, and one tinted green to knock down glare. An audio cord comes from the back of the helmet and gets plugged into the console. Inside the helmets are pads to spread the weight, and soft cones to cover your ears and aid hearing.

The military allows you to paint your name, unit insignia, and most anything you want on your helmet's back and sides. The helmets are comfortable, lightweight, easily carried, and our most important piece of equipment. We were now ready to fly.

With a great deal of anticipation, we boarded a green Army bus and headed to the main heliport. Aviation fuel and the loud thrum of whirring rotor blades filled our senses. We entered the building and were led to A-2 training room.

There were 10 tables and 10 instructor pilots awaiting us. Each instructor was assigned three students. I was assigned to Mr. B., an employee of Southern Airways.

Southern Airways was hired by the Army to fill in for instructors who were sent to Vietnam.

During pre-flight classes, we'd learned about helicopters. Our classes included basic helicopter principles, mechanics, aerodynamics, weather forecasting, navigation, and pre and post-flight checks.

OH-23 controls

Mr. B. led his three new charges to the flight line. It was time to put some of our book learning to use. The flight line was filled with Hiller OH-23D Ravens – 3-man observation aircrafts converted for flight school. He had us climb atop the aircraft, where we became familiar with the rotor system and the safety checks we needed to perform. There are several control rods, many cotter pins, and safety wires to be checked before each flight.

We took turns in the cockpit, handling the cyclic (which controls horizontal motion), collective (which controls vertical motion), and pedals (which control tail rotor pitch.) The feel of the controls was exhilarating, though we never left the ground.

As I moved the controls, he pointed out what was happening to the helicopter. The rotor blade changed pitch—its angle—as the collective was pulled up, then became level again as the collective was lowered. When I moved the cyclic forward, the blades moved forward. They followed my movements as I moved the cyclic right, left, and back. My peers outside saw the pitch on the tail rotor change as I moved the foot pedals. It was all quite extraordinary!

Not far from the heliport was a large, open field. The instructors would take us there to learn how to hover.

When my turn came, Mr. B. flew us to the field, set the aircraft down, and talked me through the elements of hovering.

Hover practice

He pointed out the altimeter, compass, and rotor RPM dials. He made sure to note the warning marks. The green area noted the optimum RPM. The red area was less than optimal. At the top of the red were large letters that said VNE: "velocity never to exceed." Most pilots called it "very near eternity." If you get to or passed that mark, the retreating blade will pass its stops, and catch the lead rotor. Rotor snap! Down you go in a twisted mass of metal!

Mr. B. demonstrated the use of the controls as he brought us to a hover. He had me put my hands and feet on the controls, and when he felt I had the principles down, he said, "You've got it. Keep it in the state of Texas." I snickered under my breath.

Of all the things I've ever done, learning how to hover was the most physically and emotionally and draining thing I've ever experienced.

The aircraft went left. As I strained to correct, we went up, right, down, and then started to turn. The RPM went up and then down, as I fought the motorcycle-style throttle.

My hands, feet, and arms were moving as fast as I could move them. An hour later (actually a few seconds), Mr. B. said, "I've got it!" and regained control.

I slumped back in the seat. My head was spinning and my shirt was drenched in sweat, but we were still "in the state of Texas." Barely!

The bus ride back to the barracks was nearly silent. Most of us were sound asleep! I'm not sure any of us went to lunch that day.

I must have lost several pounds those first few weeks, battling that heartless metal monster.

I finally learned fighting was futile; the mastery of the machine came through finesse.

My college golf instructor once told me, "You're holding the club too tight; hold it like you're holding a baby bird." That's how you fly a helicopter – gently, relaxed, and with delicate movements.

We still had class in the afternoon, but the teachers understood our tendency to doze, at least the first few days.

Flight school is tedious with lots of repetition. You practice and practice until you have each skill mastered.

The next major hurdle, after learning to hover, was flying solo. We practiced at several stage fields west of Mineral Wells.

After two weeks, Mr. B. told me to hover over to the tower and land. As he was leaving the aircraft, he said, "Take it around three times and meet me back here."

Excitement, pride, and a large helping of fear flushed through my body as I hovered towards the takeoff pad. I contacted the tower to inform them I was flying solo. Tower cleared me for takeoff, I applied power, and my whole world changed as the ground slowly fell away.

Three times around the practice field: takeoff, reach 300 feet, turn left and climb to 500, turn downwind, ride past the field, turn base and start my descent, turn final, and line up with the landing pad, descend to a hover. One down, two to go.

Stage field

On the way home, the bus pulled over at a local motel, which had a swimming pool. If you've ever soloed, you know what's coming. All new soloing students are thrown into the pool, clothes on! This tradition is fun, especially if it's hot and you don't forget to take your boots off. I forgot! They quickly filled with water.

As I sank to the bottom of the pool, the deep end of course, I was glad I had remembered to take a deep breath. After trying unsuccessfully to swim, I walked across the bottom of the pool, climbed the ladder, emptied my boots, and got back on the bus.

The final major hurdle in Basic Flight School is autorotation – landing without your engine running! Helicopters have a unique design that allows the aircraft to return to earth gently if the engine fails. When the throttle is rapidly turned to idle or the engine fails, the transmission immediately disconnects. Of course, "gently" depends on the pilot remaining in control and being trained in autorotation.

The most important part of that training is to remember to lower the collective, the vertical flight control. This moves the rotor blade to a flat, neutral position, allowing the downward movement of the aircraft to force the rotors to continue to spin.

You are taught autorotation, at a hover, early in training. Autorotation from regular flight is another problem altogether. Your instructor will reach over to the throttle and disconnect your engine. You've been drilled on what to say and do:

1. Lower the collective for powerless flight.
2. Turn the aircraft into the wind.
3. Pick a safe landing spot and descend as carefully as possible.
4. Make a distress call, giving location and situation.

The real test comes as your instructor says, "Hover over to the tower." Yikes!

If you think flying solo is a real thriller, consider being 500 feet above the runway and turning off your own engine. Double yikes!

Euphoria is often balanced with a downer. My downer came not long after my solo. I was ordered to report to headquarters, no explanation. The sergeant announced me to the colonel, and I came to attention in front of his desk.

The next 20 minutes, I stood at attention as he yelled at me. He not only yelled at me, he yelled at all warrant officer candidates. I am convinced he was not happy with his job, or was under some kind of stress.

That afternoon, when I reported to Mr. B., he asked if I understood why I had been called to H.Q. I explained what happened and that I still didn't know why I was there. He smiled as he told me I had forgotten to sign my log book. Never did that again!

Having passed Basic skills and survived "Weeding, part 1," our flight moved onto Advanced Basic.

CHAPTER FOUR
I'M REALLY DOING THIS

Advanced Basic Flight Training consists of navigation and field maneuvers, which include cross-country flights, landing on uneven ground, instrument, and formation flying.

The trickiest maneuver was formation flying. Part of our ground school included instruction on formation flying: how close and at what position we should be, communication with the flight, and how to make turns, climbs, and descents.

Instructors had gone over what to do if we were in formation and had to make an emergency break up. We had practiced this break up on several occasions. The lead ship would climb, the right flank would break right, and left flank would go left.

The back half of the formation would do the same, except the lead would descend, as would his wing ships, while they broke right or left.

As with any other skill, it started with our instructors flying with us. Then we would team with another instructor and his student, and practice flying circles, figure eights, climbs, descents, takeoffs, and landings.

Formation flying was important, since infantry units moved together, by helicopter. It was all done in formation with as many as a dozen in a single formation. The helicopters needed to land close together, so they could quickly form as a fighting unit.

As we mastered the skills, the instructors would add us, as solos, until we had groups as large as six aircrafts.

On one of these training missions, we had formed up several miles from any air traffic; it was a six-aircraft formation, which included four solo students. The lead aircraft began making gentle turns, descents, and climbs. He had noticed a small fixed-wing aircraft moving in our direction, and made course corrections accordingly.

We were all watching our distance and positioning, when the lead ship suddenly yelled, "Break! Break! Break!"

Our formation broke up, as the small fixed-wing flew right where we had been. He had missed us only because our lead ship had been alert and followed procedure. What the aircraft was doing, we never knew; he had flown out of our vision and disappeared.

Solo cross-country navigation is fun – no instructors, just a fellow student reading the map and giving the pilot adjustments to his route. We would start from the heliport, or staging grounds, and navigate to a destination predetermined by our instructor. We were given pre-flight weather conditions, maps, and aircraft assignments.

It was an amazing feeling floating above the flat Texas landscape, with farms, cows, and gently-flowing streams below. Military maps often show farm buildings, but their accuracy cannot always be counted on. You need to follow roads, rivers, and line-of-sight navigation. Line of sight means you pick out large navigation aids, such as cities and mountains, and line them up with your destination.

Once we arrived at our destination, we would land, change places, and navigate home.

Night navigation is a lot harder; it's dark out there with no visual navigational aids, only our compass and a red map-reading light.

The Army had learned that a red light allows a pilot to read his map while not affecting his night vision. Each military pilot is issued a flashlight that contains a white and red lens.

We usually flew in groups, trail formation. This allowed for easier location if there was an accident or incident. We received preflight instructions from our safety officer. He would give us our destination, wind speed, and direction, what type of landing we would be making, which airport, dirt field, or landing pad, our aircraft assignment, and who we were flying with.

On a long-distance night flight from Mineral Wells to Abilene, Texas, my first in-flight emergency occurred. Halfway to Abilene, David was flying and I was navigator. We heard a loud "pop!" We both looked to see if the rotor blades were still there. Yikes!

Suddenly we started down. My pilot lowered the collective and turned into the wind. We couldn't see the ground, but we knew the dark spots were trees and the lighter spots, open area or water.

At 500 feet, we didn't have much time to think. He picked a large light spot and, praise the Lord, found an open, flat cow pasture.

He had flipped on the landing light, and we were blinded by its reflection on the windshield! I stuck my head between my legs as low as I could to see out the aircraft's chin bubble, and suddenly saw the ground rushing up. I yelled, "FLARE! FLARE! FLARE!"

Flare is the word used to describe the last action used to decelerate or stop your descent. That action consists of pulling the cyclic back into your chest and rapidly pulling the collective all the way up.

David pulled back the cyclic, popped the collective, and we landed softly on the dark Texas soil!

He told me later he never saw the ground till after we landed. Thank you, Lord!

We both looked over our downed aircraft, and David flipped off the aircraft's electrical system and shut the engine down.

I remember looking up and seeing the lights of our flight making a big circle above us. It was a very comforting sight.

A few minutes later our chase aircraft, a much larger turbine powered helicopter, called and told us to turn our lights back on. They landed nearby and questioned what had happened.

The maintenance officer first thought we had made a precautionary landing. Having dealt with numerous incidences involving student pilots, he was quick to go with the easiest explanation. After we explained the engine was running, but the rotor wasn't turning, he changed his mind. It just isn't possible!

When starting a helicopter's engine, the rotor begins turning immediately. The transmission is tied directly to the rotor shaft.

Maintenance would not allow the downed craft to be left alone, so a coin was flipped and I left for Abilene. We had to make sure our flight arrived in Abilene and then made it home safely.

David told me later it was dark and very scary being alone in the cold Texas night. He had heard a sound, but there was no moon, so he couldn't tell what it was. His head filled with numerous thoughts, one of which was cows, particularly bulls. He immediately climbed up to the rotor mast and held on tight. It wasn't long before a deer jumped over the tail, and disappeared into the night. About that time the maintenance helicopter arrived and secured the downed aircraft and its lonely pilot.

They rigged a sling around the downed helicopter, and transported it, and its young pilot, back to Wolters.

Several weeks later, our flight commander received the maintenance report on our downed craft. The transmission on a helicopter is filled with gears and rods. They work similarly to an automobile transmission; however, they have one complicating factor: one set of rods controls the movement of the rotor mast.

According to the maintenance department, one of the control rods had broken and shot through the reduction gears, bringing the aircraft down.

The day after the report arrived, David and I were called in front of the flight class. The flight commander stood us at attention and began berating us in front of our peers, telling everyone we hadn't followed procedures and had made a mess of a perfectly good helicopter.

I looked at my fellow pilot, David, who was clutching his fist and looking confused. All of a sudden, the entire instructor team burst out laughing. The commander told us to relax, and then told the whole flight how proud he was of us. Unbeknownst to us, my intercom, which should have communicated just to my pilot, had broadcast to everyone on the channel. It had been recorded back at Wolters and a written record sent to our flight commander.

He reminded the flight that working together was the key to success, and we had displayed the ultimate in teamwork. We had a true emergency, worked together, and survived. He thanked us for not destroying his perfectly good helicopter.

The last of the "weeding" occurred during instrument training. I had to learn to fly by instruments only. This involved simulators. They acted like real helicopters but couldn't leave the ground. The instrument panel and controls were identical to the ones on the helicopters.

I had to squeeze into a single-seat, cramped simulator and put on a hood that looked like a welder's mask. It didn't allow me to see anything but the panel. As I moved the controls, the simulator would move just as the aircraft would. It was actually fun, at least for awhile.

A video was playing on the simulator's screen, and I had to react to it. We flew a complete flight, from takeoff to landing. Along the route, some kind of incident would occur that required me to practice a newly-learned skill. The engine might quit, a sudden cross wind might take me off course, or I might be hit by a rainstorm. After half an hour, I was mentally exhausted.

The real instrument training began when it was time to actually fly. My instructor had me hover to the takeoff pad and put on a hood. Again, I could only see the instrument panel. He instructed me to inform the tower I was doing an instrument takeoff. After I was cleared, I concentrated on the instruments, added power, and started my climb.

I cannot fully explain how it felt to leave the ground totally blind and dependent on a set of dials. I have a greater respect for a "seeing eye dog" and the courage of its sightless owner.

I followed my instructor's guidance, as far as direction, altitude, and avoiding other aircraft. After receiving several good tongue lashings for not correctly monitoring the instruments, I made up my mind I was going to be perfect next time.

The next day I followed his directions to a T. He had me fly in a holding pattern. This was where my main problem had been. I was making perfect turns, and controlling my airspeed. I just knew he was going to congratulate me on a "job well done!"

My head started hurting as I continued to make perfect circles in the clear Texas sky.

Finally, I asked him to take the controls, as my head was really hurting. He said, "You want to know why your head is hurting? Look at the altimeter!"

I couldn't believe my eyes. I had been making perfect circles alright, but they had been "corkscrew" circles. I had started at 500 feet and failed to realize I had not checked my altimeter. I was now at 2,500 feet! Fortunately for me, he took us back down to 500 feet and let me try again. This time I was perfect. I had passed the last "weeding" test at Fort Wolters, Texas.

I was now a real helicopter pilot. I really could do it!

I cannot give you an exact figure on how many were "weeded," but 282 helicopter pilots graduated from Basic Flight School and headed to Fort Rucker, Alabama for Advanced Training.

It was mid October, 1966.

CHAPTER FIVE
HIDE-AND-SEEK

One of my favorite kid games was hide-and-seek.

At Bethel Christian Academy, when I first entered school, there were just four primary-level students – three girls and me.

I was the youngest, so Susan, Muriel, and Diane always made me be "it." We played in a large classroom that was used for storage. There were lots of hiding places among the boxes, furniture, and office equipment. We were young and it was fun!

"Escape and evasion" was what the military called it. We did not enjoy being "found." We practiced dressing in camouflage and hiding among the trees and bushes. We also hunted for others who were hiding from us. Fort Rucker was a huge fort and offered diverse areas for practicing many different skills. There were large oak thickets, scrub trees, and bushes of many types. Large open fields with tall grass and brush offered abundant opportunities to improve our skills. This place was a hide-and-seek heaven.

I remember the cold, dry February day our company loaded into an olive drab Army truck. It dropped us off at a large, open, windswept field. It was on the side of a hill with a beautiful view. The grass was turning brown, but the green fir trees that surrounded the field made for a serene pastoral scene.

We were in groups of 10; each group was given a burlap bag of supplies. We had an area map, a small pot, one pound of rice, a dead chicken, and some water. They told us it was going to be a long and cold night, so cook and eat what was in the bag. This was all the nourishment we would get.

There would be a signal to start the exercise.

We collected enough dry material to get a fire going. The water was just starting to boil when gunfire started us moving, straight down the hill.

It was early November, so we were dressed in cold weather fatigues, including our heavy jackets. It was definitely going to freeze. The sky was clear, no rain or snow in sight. Thank you, Lord!

I had control of the map and a decent sense of direction, so I led the way. I knew our current position and a red "X" marked the spot, 10 miles away, where a helicopter would come to our "rescue."

We had gone several miles, headed for a river with a bridge clearly marked on the map, when someone in our group decided we were going the wrong way. I argued we weren't. After a heated discussion, he suggested we go a different direction, so off we went. I kept telling him we were heading away from the bridge, and there was nothing where we were going but trees and cold river water.

An hour later, deep in the Alabama wilderness, the group finally decided I just may have been right. The discussion then was whether we should attempt to go back and find the bridge, or just try and cross the river. We were growing tired, and an hour or more hike back to the bridge was quickly losing out to the river-fording plan.

We weren't sure how deep the water was, so we sent the "wrong-way leader" across first. He was 6 foot 3, and around 230 pounds – a lot bigger than the rest of us, so it was only fair.

He was halfway across, and the water was only up to his waist, so we removed our pants and boots and fell in behind. The water was COLD! Reaching the other side, I dried off with my pants and jacket. I wrung out my underwear, and nearly froze putting them back on.

We were finally headed in the right direction. The fact that we were off course meant we were outside our enemy's hunting zone, so our chattering teeth and vocal complaints wouldn't draw their attention.

Our "wrong-way leader" was still point man, when we suddenly found ourselves facing a green barricade. A large tree, and several bushes, blocked our way to the walking trail that would lead us to our pickup point.

Our leader quickly assessed the problem, and grabbed the nearest limb. As he pulled the limb up and out of his way, there was a cacophony of sound that sent him in full retreat, yelling, "Bear! Bear!"

His retreat left all nine of his fellow warriors sprawled in his wake. Being close behind our leader, I was one of the first to reap his terror. I was also one of the first to notice the "bear" had feathers, and was in fact a very large, very irritated turkey that had been unceremoniously roused from his slumber.

After corralling our "bear" hunter, and checking our bumps and bruises, we stopped for the night, and settled under the "bear" tree. It was late and we were tired. The "bear" adrenaline had finally run its course.

It was a restless night as the cold crept slowly across our unprotected bodies. No blankets, no fire, no tent, just 10 wet, smelly bodies, lying close together, trying to get warm.

I tossed and turned most of the night. The ground was hard, and my bottom half was still wet and cold.

As dawn lightened the sky, I became aware my legs were resisting any movement. A closer investigation revealed a thin layer of ice covering my fatigue pants. I stood up and brushed off the ice.

There was no possibility of a fire; we had no matches or dry material. Our only recourse was to start moving. It was a painful event – every muscle in my body screamed as I roused them to action.

Our map showed us to be only a few miles from our goal. As one, we struggled forward, closer and closer to a hot meal and dry clothes.

An hour later, a yell from our front brought us to a halt. The "enemy" had spotted us. We attempted to hide, but blackberry bushes were our only serious cover. No thanks!

A squad of "enemy" soldiers quickly surrounded us and took us to a holding cage. The cage was large enough to hold 20 or 30, but there was still no heat. I thought it strange the helicopter pad was right next to the cage. I guess there was no winning this game of hide-and-seek!

A medical officer came to inspect us, and quickly concluded we needed to be warmed and dried. He had us moved to a large room with a nice warm fire. There were soup and sandwiches. After an hour of warmth and a hot meal, a helicopter picked us up and carried us back to our barracks.

Hide-and-seek, military style, was over. We lost, but we had learned some important lessons. Things were not going to be as controlled in a combat zone, but we could be better prepared.

Keeping dry is of major importance, and carrying nourishment that did not need to be heated was wise.

You would think hide-and-seek in a helicopter would be one-sided. The noise of our helicopter would aid the enemy and put us at a disadvantage. However, we were taught to use our environment to hide us. We could spring from behind trees or buildings to surprise the enemy. They actually showed us movies of aircraft using those techniques. I used this training quite often when I was on the "seek" in Vietnam.

Fort Rucker was used for transitioning rookie helicopter pilots into pilots of much larger turbine-powered aircrafts. We practiced many of the skills we had learned in the smaller helicopters. We needed to learn how to autorotate the larger aircraft. There were quite a few more engine and navigational instruments to keep track of and this aircraft needed a much larger area to land.

We practiced skills we would need in a combat zone: formation flying, low-level navigation, hillside landings, repelling, rope recovery, load lifting, and artillery targeting.

Formation flying

Our company spent weeks in simulated combat conditions, flying miles from base camp. We would land on grass runways and sleep in tents close to our aircraft. These landing areas created their own problems. They were not on level ground. Turbine-powered aircraft use JP4 for fuel, which releases fumes that settle in low spots.

Unless these fumes are blown away, they sit and accumulate. They are highly volatile! We were warned not to light a match or smoke anywhere near our aircraft. If anyone was standing in a low area and there had been no breeze, his life was in real danger.

I've watched TV movies that show jet helicopters crash and explode in a fireball. This would never happen. JP4 must be vaporized to burn or explode. No fireballs. Sorry, Hollywood!

We had several aircraft with tactical armament. I remember flying to the gun range and firing live rounds and rockets from these powerful, airborne gun platforms. Little did I know how important these short hours of training would be to my Vietnam experience!

Loading ammo for practice in the field

The most interesting missions were low-level navigation. On several of our aircraft we had local maps on rollers. There was a machine with a long needle that moved as the aircraft flew. Just before takeoff, we set the needle to point to our current location.

As the instructor and his student prepared to take off, the second student would be sitting on a jump seat just behind the machine. The machine was stationed on a small platform between and behind the two pilots.

The second student communicated to the student pilot where the needle was pointing: "There should be a farm on the left." "Are we flying next to a highway off to our right?" "Are we crossing a river right now?" If what the pilot was seeing didn't match what the map was showing, the second student would move the needle to the correct spot.

We were testing an early GPS. It was terrible! The rollers either turned fast, or not at all, which caused the needle to jump around the map, rendering the machine useless. I've used several types of GPS models; the best so far is on my phone.

The scariest part of Rucker's training was hillside landings. We would hover next to a hill and ground our skid against it. Often the hill was steep so we had to ensure our rotor blades were well above the top of the rise.

When no landing spot was available, ropes were used to repel troops and supplies to the ground. This skill could come in handy when there was enemy fire, and a quick getaway was necessary.

Most large helicopters are equipped with a load hook on the bottom center of the aircraft. If we were going to lift a net that contained cargo, the crew chief would slip under the aircraft, release the hook, attach the net loops, and refasten the hook.

On one training mission, as I approached the drop point, the crew chief, in this case the second student pilot, guided me over the spot where I was to drop the load. He watched the drop master on the ground who guided us to the right spot and made sure we were low enough not to cause damage to the load. When the crew chief student told me to drop the load, I pushed a button on the cyclic and the hook opened releasing the load.

The key to the whole process was to listen to my crew chief, and ensure the load did not start swinging. It's difficult enough flying with a load; a swinging load throws off the balance of the aircraft. Too big a swing and you must jettison the load or the cable could tangle with the main or tail rotor.

During the Civil War, artillery spotters were in baskets under large balloons. These balloons were tethered to the ground and could be raised and lowered as needed. Their job was to watch where artillery shells landed and let the artillery commander know where to and how to adjust his fire. The balloonist had paper and a bag of rocks. If his instructions could not be heard, he would write them down, tie them to a rock, and drop them to a handler. I'm glad we had radios; that rock stuff could be dangerous from 500 feet!

Maps were universal for our military. They were divided into little squares that represented 1-kilometer by 1-kilometer areas. These squares were called "klicks."

We received book training, as well as hands-on training in artillery adjustment. We were taught the same tactical language used by the artillery batteries: "klicks," "adjust fire" (give instructions to pinpoint [usually one round] or change the point of impact), "fire for effect," (have one battery fire no more than six rounds), and "commence fire" (all batteries fire at will).

Fort Rucker has a large area dedicated to artillery practice. We would fly to the target area, contact fire control, and give them target coordinates and request "adjust fire" (one round). The practice rounds are smoke markers. After the round lands, you give fire control new coordinates, or give them "klick" instructions: one "klick" right, two "klicks" up, whatever is needed. After fire control acknowledges, we again requested "adjust fire" (one round).

During training, I was given three practice rounds. I was graded according to how close the rounds were to the target and how clear my instructions were. I passed!

Our class work continued at Fort Rucker. Other than studying the workings of turbine-powered aircraft and local weather, we were learning about Vietnam, its people, and customs.

There were also interviews with the FBI. My parents, brother, pastor, and many of my friends were interviewed before I received my "secret clearance," required to fly military aircraft in sensitive areas.

Several times my flight was ushered into a secure room, where we presented our IDs and signed papers promising not to divulge anything we were about to see or hear. After completing all the paperwork, we viewed secret military movies, most of which you may see, from time to time, on television. I still can't tell you everything I saw and heard. I promised.

I felt important, until I was on leave. My dad had the news on and they were showing one of the same top-secret movies I had seen in that little dark room several weeks earlier.

Fort Rucker was intense, but did not have the stress of Fort Wolters. I had 110 hours of flight time under my belt before arriving at Rucker. I was a pilot! Nothing could match the stress of my first moments trying to hover, fly solo, or shutting off my own engine and riding that beast all the way to the ground.

At Rucker we didn't get harassed and we got passes to leave the base. We got to drive to Florida and enjoy the beaches. We began to actually feel like military officers. The closer to graduation, the more we were treated like officers.

Having officers' bars and wings pinned on my uniform after an impressive graduation ceremony and parade was something to remember. On the afternoon of March 14, 1967, I became a warrant officer helicopter pilot in the United States Army! It was a thrill and an honor.

MARCH 14, 1967 Graduation Day Ft. Rucker, AB

George   Doug   Rob   Larry

The military has a tradition: upon receiving our first set of bars as a new officer, I needed to have a new five-dollar bill on my person.

When I received my first salute, I was to return the salute and present the bill to the saluting soldier.

At graduation, an enterprising sergeant stationed himself at the front door. As we new officers filed out of the ceremony, he saluted and held out his left hand. He easily made 300 dollars in less than half an hour. Long live military tradition!

Before I left Fort Rucker, I was given my next assignment: Vietnam, the 11th Armored Cavalry Regiment, and two weeks' leave.

I am undecided about the justification for the war and its final outcome. I can only look to God and what he tells his children: "Render unto Caesar the things that are Caesar's, and unto God the things that are God's" (Mark 12:17).

I would not change a thing. Running away would have solved nothing. I believe I honored the Lord in all that I did.

CHAPTER SIX:
GETTING THERE (VIETNAM PART 1)

I left Travis Air Force Base, Vacaville, California, on March 29, 1967.

My parents and fiancée brought me to Travis the morning of March 28th. I presented my papers to the gate guards and we were sent to the intake center.

My family followed me around for the next hour as I received vaccinations and picked up my orders. With all the formalities completed, the flight master sent me to the flight line to board my plane.

I kissed and hugged my family goodbye and watched as they headed home. I would not see them again for nearly a year! It was a bright, sunny California day.

After waiting several hours at flight control, we were informed there was a typhoon in our flight path, so we would be staying in the States one more night. The flight master issued food and sleeping vouchers, and arranged transportation to a local motel. There were 45 officers and enlisted men scheduled for our flight.

Vacaville in 1967 was not as big (population then: 10,898) and busy as it is today (population now: 98,510). It was a sleepy bedroom community for the San Francisco Bay Area. It did not have much in the way of excitement, but it did provide good food and a quiet retreat for the many active duty Air Force personnel assigned to Travis Airbase.

That night I roomed with Rob, Larry, and George, three of my best flight school friends. We enjoyed steak dinners—on the U.S. Air Force—at the local steak house. Glad we were delayed!

We were all headed to Vietnam, but not to the same unit. My orders said the 11th Armor. Rob was going to the 1st Infantry. We served our whole tour in those units; many of our flight had their orders changed upon arrival in country, due to unit needs.

Air Force Transportation picked us up the next afternoon, and delivered us back to the flight line. After a short wait in the sparse military terminal, we boarded a chartered TWA 707 airliner bound for Binh Hoa Air Force Base, Vietnam. The plane was a stripped-down version of the civilian model, no first class seats. We did have stewardesses, civilian pilots, and really good in-flight meals.

Five hours later, we landed in Honolulu, Hawaii, at Hickam Air Force Base. Stepping off the plane at dusk, I was struck by the high humidity, common in Hawaii. Unfortunately, since it was only a fuel stop, I didn't get to see any of the lush, green islands. It was my first time on the Islands, but fortunately not my last, thanks to my oldest daughter Lisa!

We had another island stop on our refuel list, but where it was, I'm not sure. As we prepared for landing, the pilot came on the intercom and told us, "Put away your cameras, lower your window shades, and keep them down until we come to a final stop." I just had to peek!

The island was beautiful in the early morning sun. One end rested on a beautiful, white sandy beach, touched by azure-blue waters. The island rose gradually until it reached a hundred-foot drop-off. The waves lapped gently against the golden-brown cliffs.

There was a beachside village lined with palm trees; halfway between the cliff and the beach, the runway ran down the center of the island. It looked so peaceful.

Along the edge of the runway were rows of U-2 spy planes. Their long, slender body and needle-pointed nose set them apart from all other aircraft. However, the real thrill came as we continued down the runway. Mixed among the U-2s were a series of beautiful, sleek, black, twin-engine aircraft. I had no idea what I was seeing. Very few would! They were SR-71 Blackbirds, America's most secret spy planes. In 1967 no one knew these planes existed.

Manila, Philippines was next on the landing list. We were there just long enough to refuel. I can't tell you anything about the Philippines – we weren't allowed off the plane.

20 plus hours after departing sunny California, we arrived in Long Binh, Vietnam. It had been a long and tiring trip.

I spent three days at the Armed Forces intake center, waiting for my unit to pick me up. They would take me to Blackhorse, 11th Armor's base camp. I got a real education awaiting their arrival.

The buses the Army used had woven wire fencing over the windows; we learned later the fencing was there so no one could throw a hand grenade into the bus.

While riding one of those buses, I observed a woman, I believed to be in her 80s, pull up her dress and pee next to the sidewalk. I wasn't in Kansas anymore! Turns out the woman was actually in her 30s and on "beetle nut," a locally grown drug, which makes your teeth turn black and decay. It also wrinkles your skin. Welcome to Vietnam! These people have known nothing but war since birth, and it has taken its toll.

On the third day, I was picked up by an 11th Cav helicopter and flown across the dark green jungle to my new assignment.

The 11th Armored Cavalry Regiment had arrived in Vietnam in September 1966; they landed at Vung Tau Sea Port, and moved to Xuan Loc, where they established Blackhorse Base Camp. It was carved out of the jungle alongside the road that ran from Vung Tau to Bien Hoa airbase. It was an hour trip, by tank, either direction.

Xuan Loc was a small farming village five miles up the road towards Bien Hoa. Red dirt, scrub trees, and jungle surrounded three sides of our camp. They left scrub trees and bamboo thickets spread around, inside the perimeter, just to keep the dust down and add a little color other than red.

They had been in country less than six months when I arrived.

The regiment's battle components consisted of 1st, 2nd, and 3rd Squadrons, and Air Cav Troop. The three squadrons were broken into troops of M48 Patton tanks and 11th Cav (designed) A-CAVs (armed personnel carriers with two mounted .60-caliber machine guns on the rear sides, and a .50-caliber in the front).

The 11th Cav was designed to search and destroy and was fully equipped to handle the task.

Air Cav Troop had three platoons of gunships, the largest gunship company in Vietnam, and one platoon of "slicks," empty aircrafts used to transport people and supplies.

All helicopters, including slicks, had door gunners armed with hard-mounted M60 machine guns.

Most units had the door guns hung on bungee cords. Several had tail rotors shot off, pilots wounded, and main rotors damaged by their own guns; the bungee cords were unstable and bounced the guns around.

After replacing several tail rotors, and having pilots nearly hit by rounds from their door guns, one of our officers designed a hard mount for the M60 door guns. It had been dangerous to have your elbow out the window!

The mount was firmly attached to the aircraft. Three swivels, with stops, allowed the gun to move in all directions. The stops kept rounds from hitting the tail, or main rotor. It also protected the pilots, and allowed the gunners to safely lean out to fire under the flying craft.

When I arrived, all the 11th's aircraft were hard mounted, thank you, Lord! It was nice knowing I didn't have to worry about my door gunner accidently killing me!

11th armor base camp, Blackhorse, Xuan Loc, Vietnam

Our gunships, all C models with extra-large rotor blades, were of three types, evenly divided among the three platoons. One type had four M60 side-mounted machine guns and two rocket pods, each holding seven 2.75-inch folding fin aerial rockets. Another had two rocket pods holding 48 rockets we called a HOG. The third held a nose-mounted 40mm grenade launcher with the nickname FROG.

The slicks were all D models with longer, thinner bodies and rotors. Everything that could be painted was painted Army green.

Arriving at our base camp, I was ushered to headquarters where I turned in my transfer papers. I was informed that I was being assigned to 2nd Platoon to replace a pilot who had rotated home.

2nd Platoon was a gunship platoon. Our C models were heavy duty aircraft, with double hydraulics. We were in a hot, high humidity country and the laws of aerodynamics were being fully tested. Heavy air, heavy aircraft, and heavy loads were a recipe for disaster. Aircraft like light air, light weight, and light loads.

The double hydraulics gave us some extra protection from lethal gunfire. If one set of hydraulics is shot out or disabled, the second will give you a chance to land safely. Lighter helicopters become sluggish if you lose hydraulics, but they can still be flown.

In the middle of my tour, one of our C models lost both sets of hydraulics. Fortunately, they had just begun landing procedures and were descending slowly. If it had been the reverse, they would have been unable to stop the climb. When skids touched down, they shut off the engine and saved the aircraft; they did have to replace the two bent cyclics. This was another of God's incredible miracles.

Before my first day at Blackhorse ended, I was sent to the clinic where I was given three containers of malaria pills, one for each type of malaria found at my new home.

One vial contained 365 of the larger orange-colored pills, one for each day. The second and third contained 12 pills each, one per month. The doctor informed me I was now in the heart of malaria country. Every type of malaria known to man can be found in the jungles surrounding Blackhorse Base Camp, Xuan Loc, Vietnam.

A private, in his olive drab Army jeep, drove me to my tent. Home consisted of a six-man green canvas tent surrounded by eight layers of gray sand bags.

We had a full-size refrigerator and a black and white TV. Yes! "Good morning, Vietnam!" was real! There were six army cots and six storage lockers with drying lights. The drying lights kept our spare clothes from rotting from the humidity.

I asked my fiancée for some baby powder—clothes weren't the only thing rotting—and she sent me four large cans. She's so wonderful!

There was one last thing I needed to do before I could join my flight team. I had to pick up new fire-retardant flight suits, a bulletproof vest, and a pair of dull green jungle boots. The flight suits were a dingy brown but quite comfortable. The vest had fiberglass plates, front and back; they could stop a direct hit from a .50-caliber round.

When I flew, I took the back plate out and put it under my seat. The seats in a C model are also bulletproof, except the seat bottom, thus the back plate under the seat.

Jungle boots were very comfortable in hot, humid weather – they had leather bottoms and nylon-webbed tops. They kept out the water but allowed the boot to breath and kept our feet cool. Changing our socks three or four times a day also helped.

Well, I was finally here – 7,000 miles and 14 time zones away from home. It took a long time getting here. I just needed to get used to the heat, humidity, mosquitoes, dust, mud, and getting shot at.

I was ready to meet the rest of my new platoon and go on my first mission.

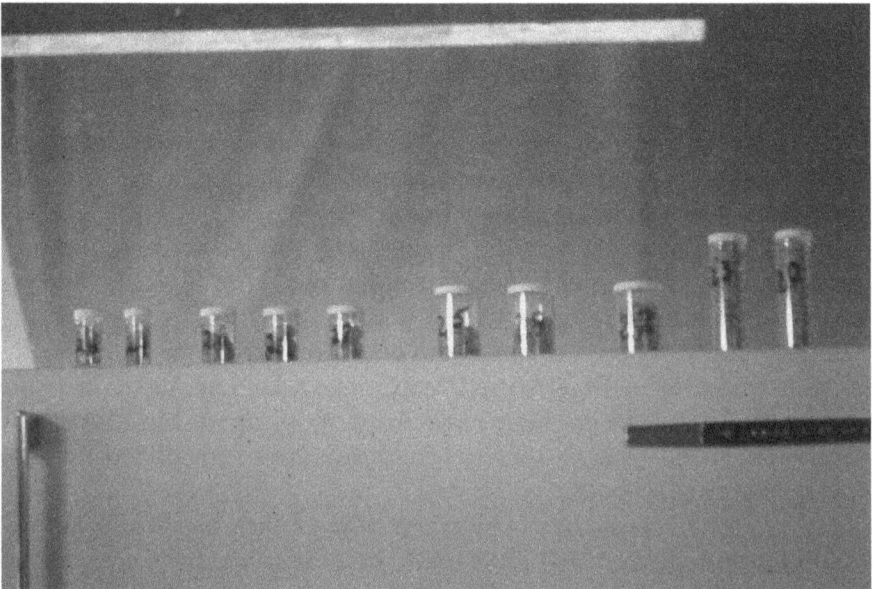

Malaria pills (you start with 52, and take 1 pill a week)

CHAPTER SEVEN
PREPARING FOR BATTLE (VIETNAM PART 2)

The private, in his dull green Army jeep, was waiting outside the quartermaster's. His assignment was to take me and my load of combat gear back to 2nd Platoon's officer's tent.

As we drove along, I noticed everything was covered in a fine reddish-brown dust. The same color I had seen as we approached Blackhorse from the air.

The airfield was covered in a dark, oily substance that kept the dust down so it wouldn't be kicked up by untold aircraft, drowning Blackhorse in a swirling sea of reddish brown.

The smell of the airfield brought back old memories. As a child visiting my grandparents' home in Sarepta, Louisiana, I could

smell the railroad tracks from the other side of the dirt road. That was what I smelled here at Blackhorse airfield, right across the dirt road from my tent. It was very comforting.

My home for a year (page 57). My cot, left, and Peggy's pictures

My roommates consisted of a major, a captain, and three warrant officers. The tent was divided into two sections. The front section was our "living room." It contained an old sofa and several upholstered chairs. The focal point of the room was the black and white TV.

The tent's back three-quarters made up our bedroom. My metal army cot, with thin saggy mattress, was covered by a green rubber poncho. The poncho kept the dust off the blankets, and what were at one time white military-issue sheets. The red ochre dirt stained the white sheets and was almost impossible to bleach out.

We each had a wooden locker for our extra clothes. A 25-watt light bulb in each locker was kept on 24/7 to fight off the humidity that was trying to turn our wardrobes into green mold.

As the newest team member, I was required to fly second seat with the senior officers. Flight school had taught me the basics, but that was back in the States. There was a whole new set of tactics, maneuvers, and communications I needed to learn and practice, only this time there was an enemy with real bullets.

I flew my first mission on April 3rd, 1967.

I don't remember the mission; my flight log says it was four and a half hours and we made five landings. The last leg, through the dark Vietnamese night, was heading for home. Last legs usually meant our guns were empty.

As we headed through the night sky, I noticed these big, beautiful, shiny orange basketballs floating off to our right. Pointing this out to my aircraft commander, he informed me that between each bright orange tracer were four, .50-caliber rounds, and the shooter was searching for us.

During the Vietnam War, there were huge advancements in the use and development of helicopters. Coinciding with the offensive use, the enemy was also developing defenses. At the beginning of the war, the United States military was using Korean War-era aircraft. The enemy was also stuck in the past.

American technology was quick to respond and developed the turbine-powered helicopter, UH-1 – A, B, C, D, and E models, with each model tailored specifically for the duties they needed to perform. The C model I was flying was developed to carry advanced airborne weaponry. B, D, and E models were meant to carry personnel, equipment, and wounded.

By war's end, America had developed even more advanced weaponry and powerful helicopters. Likewise, North Vietnam was supplied more and more powerful anti-aircraft defenses by the Chinese military, starting with the .50-caliber machine guns they used against my aircraft, and later, the Chinese supplied Redeye anti-aircraft rockets and finally heat-seeking missiles.

The bottoms of our navigation lights were blacked out, so the enemy couldn't see us from the ground. They could hear the sound of our turbine engines and the thump of the rotor blades, but it was so dispersed they could not tell what direction it came from.

During the early weeks, I learned the local terrain, positions of nearby friendly units, radio procedures, which frequency contacted fire control, and which navigational aids to use. I learned tactics used by our ground units and how best to support them when they called for assistance.

I learned the terrain during morning and evening patrols. My job was to observe and let my pilot know if I saw anything out of the ordinary. Everything was out of the ordinary!

What I thought I saw from 1,000 feet when I first flew into Blackhorse was not the same as what I was seeing from 50 or 100 feet on our patrols.

The vast flat jungle was not flat; it was a series of gullies and canyons surrounded by thick foliage. There were meandering streams, sudden sharp outcrops of rock, and deep pits with cascading waterfalls.

The jungle was alive with animals, snakes, bugs, and birds. I can only imagine what dangers and beauties are hidden in that dense foliage.

I discovered a little of what was out there every time I went to the officers' club. Between my tent and the club, where I could get steaks and an occasional lobster for "free," was a large stand of golden bamboo. A dirt path led around the edge of the bamboo.

I was told, "Watch out for the local constable that guards the path." It turns out the "constable" was a cobra that sunned herself next to the trail. She would arch up when she heard us coming and then chase us down the path until we were out of her territory.

She never tried to bite us, just kept us moving. She did keep the rats and mice away, so we decided to live in harmony with nature. How's that for environmentalism!

Friendly units were easy to locate; bases were hacked out of the jungle and fortified with materials both local and brought in by truck or helicopter.

During one patrol, my pilot said, "Let's spend some of the Army's money." He had me fly to our local practice range, an old mining operation. There were rusted sheds and mining machines long abandoned. I was instructed to pick out a target and set up for a rocket attack.

He told me to pull down the $2,500 scope that hung from the roof above my head. I aligned the target with the scope's crosshairs, moved into position, and pushed the cyclic forward. As the nose lowered, the scope's crosshairs aligned with the target. I pulled the trigger built into the cyclic, and a rocket burst from its metal tube. I watched as it wobbled slightly and then began its smooth charge right where I had aimed.

My pilot took the controls, handed me a black grease pen and told me to put a small "X" on the windshield directly between the scope and where I saw the rock impact.

He had me push the scope back into place, and make another run just using the X. I was amazed when my next rocket made a direct hit right on the X. With practice, I could lead my target during a turn with the same results.

Every time we went on patrol, we made a stop at the practice range. I learned quickly it wasn't just for fun, although it was; it was about safety for our troops on the ground. They were often under attack from enemy in close proximity. I needed to be confident in my ability to pinpoint fire. Practice makes perfect!

During training we did everything through the heliport tower, or the smaller towers at the stage fields. They would clear us for takeoffs and landings, advise us about weather and air traffic, and keep us in touch with our instructors.

In Vietnam, we had Blackhorse tower to clear us for takeoffs and landings, if there was anyone on duty.

Airfield across the road

After I was airborne, if the mission was more than 50 miles from base, I contacted air traffic control. They would guide me to my destination.

If it was less than 50 miles, we would be given the frequency to contact the FAC (forward air controller) who was directing the mission. The FAC was usually in a small Army fixed-wing orbiting the battle.

If the mission was distant, I had to contact artillery radar, usually Gia Ray Mountain Artillery, if I was flying out of Blackhorse. They had control of all fire in our area. Gia Ray would clear me through any active artillery in my flight path. That stuff can really mess up your day.

Gia Ray Artillery was on the top of Gia Ray Mountain, elevation 2,700 feet; they had flattened the top and built an artillery base and control center. The mountain was 40 miles to our west.

It was isolated way up there. They were attacked on rare occasions, but it was rough, steep terrain with dense forests, waterfalls, and a very tough climb. There were no roads; everything had to be flown in.

One thing they enjoyed I couldn't: it was much cooler up there.

During flight school, our maps were local, usually covering 50 miles around our base. They were standard paper maps folded to fit our flight suit pockets.

Vietnam maps were plastic coated. We wrote radio frequencies on the larger maps that marked different artillery fire control areas. The more local maps were marked with frequencies of local units. As the co-pilot, I was the navigator. Maps were my responsibility – if we got off course it was my doing.

Things were different in Vietnam; I had to relearn how to fly. Summers in Texas and Alabama were hot and humid, but not nearly as humid as Vietnam.

I now live in Salem, Oregon; it sits on the 45th parallel, halfway between the equator and the North Pole. We have seasons here – it gets cold and it gets hot, but mostly wet.

Vietnam sits just north of the equator; its seasons are hot and dry, hotter and wet, and hottest and wettest. The same formula applies to humidity. Vietnam sits on the edge of the South China Sea, a warm body of water – the perfect setting for high humidity, severe storms, and poor flying conditions.

I did not normally carry heavy loads during training, but in Vietnam that's all we ever did. Our UH-1C gunships, with their extra-wide rotor blades, were built to carry heavy weapons and required heavy-duty hydraulics.

During the hottest weather, I couldn't add power and go; I had to "baby" the fully-loaded aircraft down the runway until I gained transitional lift, the point where a helicopter goes from hover to flight.

"Babying" meant sliding the aircraft down the runway on its thick aluminum skids until I could get to a low, forward-moving, hover.

Sliding caused the skids to overheat, and the hot aluminum smell filled the cockpit. Once I got lift, all I needed was air speed. I could then hang on as 522, my great overweight Army bird, clawed its way skyward, and we were flying.

522 in its protective spot

Once, when I was aircraft commander, we were flying from a 1st Infantry runway built in the middle of a rubber plantation. I let my rookie pilot do the takeoff. He didn't give our overweight gunship enough room to gain airspeed and pulled in too much power. We began settling into the trees.

I grabbed the controls and mowed a path through the tree tops, barely gaining enough airspeed and altitude to continue our mission. My door gunner and crew chief were yelling and complaining at the top of their lungs as the upper branches slapped their legs and arms.

One of my early missions was in support of Operation Junction City. It had started in February before I arrived. 1st and 3rd Squadrons were in a joint mission with the 1st Australian Task Force. The mission was to destroy the headquarters of the Viet Cong in Binh Duong Province.

We guarded the units as they moved along the road and supported their attacks on the dug-in enemy. Days and nights often ran together, but my knowledge of war was rapidly growing.

I played basketball in college. The longer I played, the more knowledge I gained of the game. The ball, in particular, became a source of fascination. The longer I bounced it, shot it, and passed it, the more adept I became at the game. I lay in bed at night, with my eyes closed, tossing the ball into the air above my head. My fingertips grew to know the feel and balance of the ball. My game improved the more familiar I became with the ball.

The touch and feel of the helicopter controls became my new basketball. I learned to feel and respond to the powerful aircraft's every movement. It came to the point where I didn't have to think what to do. The helicopter became attached to my brain like my arms, legs, and eyes.

The long, drawn-out mission was successful and secured routes and lines of communication between fire support bases.

I flew 18 missions that first month, a total of 46 hours of combat. Six of those missions required multiple landings for refueling and reloading.

When we were in support of units away from Blackhorse, they supplied us with food, fuel, and ammunition. Many times we spent the night in the middle of circled tanks. We had our sleeping gear but nothing to break up the hard ground under the helicopter or keep away the big, fuzzy red spiders and local snakes.

I watched as two large-rotor Chinook helicopters brought large bladders of fuel and dropped them in the circle. Some of the bladders contained aviation fuel. We used the hand pumps attached to the black rubber bladders to refuel our aircraft.

We all had tired arms pumping the handle that brought the fuel from the bladder into the hose attached to our helicopter's fuel neck. It was awhile before our fuel eater was full.

I hadn't heard from home in almost six weeks. I wrote home every day, but my mail hadn't caught up with my new address. One day the mail room delivered a pack of 30 plus letters! Letters from home, especially from one special person, kept my life in balance.

It was great to hear they were praying for me – "The effective, fervent prayer of a righteous man avails much" (James 5:16).

Between missions, I had several full days of reading and writing ahead of me. I faithfully read and answered every letter. I opened one from a friend and was surprised to find a folded cutout letter "E" stuffed in the envelope. He had written on the "E," "I was told to write you a letter. Here it is."

Don't tell anybody, but I read the letters from "my someone special" first.

I found out later the pastor had announced from the pulpit, "We should encourage our military members with letters from home." They did, and not just once. Thank you, Lord!

Operation Manhattan began in late April, eight days after the end of Junction City. 1st and 2nd Squadrons thrust into Long Nguyen Secret Zone in search of a suspected regional Viet Cong headquarters. 60 tunnel complexes were uncovered; we were told they found a number of World War I French tanks and war materials they had captured when the French Army left. Our units destroyed 1,884 fortifications, and 621 tons of rice were recovered.

This operation put a real damper on local Viet Cong operations, at least for the short term.

During my first two months, the majority of our missions involved flying cover for our unit as it moved in smaller groups doing search and destroy. We flew in close contact as our tanks and A-CAVs moved down dirt roads and across open fields, trying to make contact with the enemy and flush them from their hiding places.

As the unit made contact, we provided cover and helped drive the enemy out of their protected areas. If there were any wounded, we covered the medivac helicopters as they moved them to medical aid.

A very important lesson I learned: when landing near a village, don't turn your back on the helicopter. I was enjoying a group of children playing soccer, and didn't realize one had sneaked behind me and was trying to steal the warheads off the rockets. It would have gone unnoticed if my aircraft commander hadn't told me to turn around. He quickly shooed away the culprit and had me check the warheads – two of them were loose and ready to remove. I never let that happen again.

The children would steal anything they could get their hands on and sell it for food. It usually made its way into the hands of the enemy, who used the materials to make land mines. Often those mines killed the young thieves, or their friends, if stepped on during play.

Yes, I learned a lot my first three months. Those lessons came in handy as the pilots who taught me rotated home and I assumed the duties they had performed.

CHAPTER EIGHT
MY FIRST COMMAND (VIETNAM PART 3)

Beginning April 1967 and continuing through March 1968, running concurrent with several other operations, the 11th was issued the task called Operation Kittyhawk.

The regiment was to secure and pacify Long Khanh District. Blackhorse Base Camp is right in the middle of that district.

Three objectives were given and accomplished:

1. Keep the Viet Cong from interfering with travel on the main roads.
2. Establish areas for medical treatment (Civic Action Programs or CAP).
3. Make sure the Viet Cong did not have time to mount large offensives by harassing them on a continual basis.

During most of my tour, I flew missions supporting all these objectives. They were long, tiresome, often boring missions usually flown out of Blackhorse.

The ground units had to determine what was occurring in and around the local villages and make as many friends as possible. Without this network the mission would fail.

The medics were vital to the mission; there were no local hospitals or doctors. When the unit arrived at a village, they would meet with the elders and arrange an impromptu clinic. Nothing helped build rapport as much as helping children, the sick, and elderly.

The most memorable events occurred keeping the roads open.

The weather affected much of what could be done. December to April were the hottest and driest months, and June to August the wettest, during monsoon season.

Tanks do not function well in wet, soggy weather; they tend to bog down and dig themselves into a hole. During heavy rain, most of our units were forced to stay on main roads. Our fire teams were left to chase the enemy through the brush and mire.

My fire team was flying cover for one of our A-CAV troops, not far from base camp.

The vehicles we were protecting from our view in the air

They'd just finished a recon and C.A.P. in a local village. We'd made several circles around the troop when we heard the lead vehicle radio – he was taking fire. As we raced to the front of the column, the enemy was charging the lead vehicle.

We immediately began firing into the tree line, where the attack was coming from. Our second pass was deeper into the tree line, as the enemy ran from the scene. The brownish-green foliage was too thick to continue an accurate counterattack, but we continued sporadic fire to ensure they would continue their retreat.

The lead vehicle sustained minor damage, but remained in service. After assessing injuries and clearing the area, the column continued the short distance to base camp. We didn't hear anymore about the incident, until months later.

The after-action report concluded that the lead vehicle was unable to bring direct fire upon the enemy because they could see children chained to the enemy machine guns.

The left rear gunner had been dragged from his position on the A-CAV, and was being pulled toward the trees. The other crew members were fighting for their lives in hand-to-hand combat when our counterattack began.

With bullets landing all around, the enemy stopped their attack, released their captive and ran for the tree line.

The enemy had recently changed their strategy to hit-and-run. They had been taking major losses in previous all-out attacks.

The after-action statement recorded that if we hadn't opened fire, the young soldier was sure he would have been killed. We don't know what happened to the children; it was not included in the report.

During boring times, we watched Army TV: "Good Morning, Vietnam," news programs, and several sitcoms – "Father Knows Best," "Donna Reed," and "The Real McCoys," all in black and white. I had also purchased a set of colored pencils and a sketch pad at the commissary. My art will never hang in the Louvre, but it staved off many days of boredom.

When I was buying my art supplies, I noticed several brochures, some on automobiles and one advertising dishes. I picked up a few and took them back to my tent.

I was amazed at the prices for Noritake china straight from the factory. The military had many products that could be purchased by mail straight from the manufacturer at near cost.

I sent the brochure to my wife-to-be, who sent it back with items checked that would fit our future needs. I doubled the order, much to her surprise. We have them to this day. They came at a cost of $24: a complete 12-piece set, including tea service. Vietnam did have some perks.

I couldn't afford the Jaguar XK-E automobile, which could be delivered to my folks' house for $1,200, but I did order a top-of-the-line stereo outfit from Japan that cost me $50, delivered.

I had it shipped to my folks' house, forgetting my younger brother and his friend Frankie just might find it too tempting to ignore.

They told me later they put it together and just had to see how loud it would get. Every window in the house shook so badly they had to turn the volume down before it reached the halfway point. I wonder if I could still get that XK-E.

Often the boredom consisted of sitting and waiting for a siren to go off.

I can tell you firsthand how a fireman feels, trying to relax and go about killing time, when all of a sudden you are shocked into frightful, wide-awake alert, not knowing what's about to happen.

Each of our gunship platoons shared base camp patrol. When all three platoons were at base camp, our fire team might fly patrol once every nine days. When our platoon was alone on base camp protection, we would fly every three days!

Patrol began by flying around base camp at dawn and then again at dusk, looking for signs of enemy movement. Anything strange, we'd call fire control with the coordinates, and they'd set up artillery volleys for later that night or early morning.

We would fly tree-top level, back and forth, round and round the base camp, all eight sets of eyes looking for movement, freshly cleared areas, or anything that should not be there.

We marked places with strangely cleared areas on our laminated map with a red grease pencil. We'd look at the area again on our next patrol, or when the next team took the duty. If the clearing had a circle marked in it, usually with sticks around the edge, it would immediately be called in. The circle was used as an aiming point for a mortar position aimed at our base.

Our patrols were part of "alert team duty." When I went on "30-second alert," it would begin at dawn, when we did our first patrol. We would stay on alert until the next team relieved us at dawn.

When the alert horn went off, we had to be airborne within 30 seconds. We slept in our flight suits, flight gear always at our side or in the helicopter. Our crew slept on the aircraft's floor. Pilots slept in beds near the flight line. It was a well-programmed procedure:

1. The siren would sound.
2. The pilots would run to the aircrafts.
3. The aircraft commanders would begin starting the engines as the pilots and crews put on protective vests and helmets and tightened their seat straps. When the pilots were ready, they'd assume starting procedures as the aircraft commanders gear up.
4. When engine RPM reached flight level, the pilots began takeoff hover and informed tower.
5. With both aircraft airborne, the fire team leader contacted FAC (forward air control) and received instructions.
6.   The second team moved to "30-second alert," and the third to "five-minute."

It was possible to have all three teams in the air going to different emergencies.

If one of our tank units came under attack and needed emergency support, the "30-second" team was expected to be on station within minutes. This also applied to any other situation our command decided needed immediate attention. I was on several long-distance alerts that took us 30-40 minutes to arrive on station.

My aircraft commander and I had just finished dinner. We came off an uneventful evening patrol and were settling down for the evening. Another boring day!

Our door gunner and crew chief were heading back to the aircraft when the siren sounded. Its high-pitched scream could be heard throughout base camp.

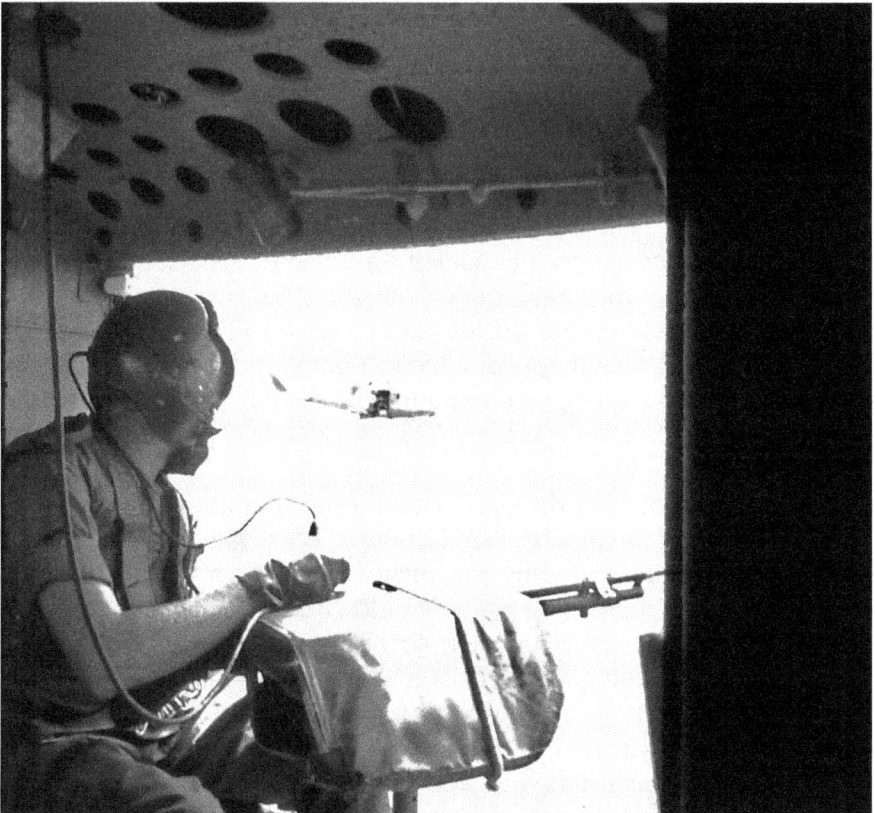

My door gunner keeping an eye on our teammate

We had refueled and were fully armed. We were ready!

Rearming after battle

I left my gear in the aircraft, so I made a beeline to my seat and began putting on my flak jacket and helmet. I buckled my safety belt and yelled to my commander, "I've got it!"

I put my left hand on the fuel control and added power. The rotor RPM came to full speed. I looked back at the crew chief, who was peering into the engine compartment. His job was to ensure there was no engine fire. He nodded "OK." I pulled in power and began hovering for takeoff.

It was dark and the only sound, other than the radio, was the roar of my rotor blades. The engine gave off a high-pitched scream that could only be dulled by earplugs – we had been told they were mandatory gear; the engine whine would cause hearing loss.

I told the tower the alert team was ready for takeoff. They cleared us and I pulled in power. We were airborne!

My aircraft commander took control of the aircraft and I contacted flight control. They informed us the South Vietnamese outpost, just to our south, was under attack with casualties. They told us to contact the American advisor on tactical channel 2.

I reached over and changed the radio to Tac 2. My commander contacted the ARVN (Army of the Republic of Vietnam) advisor and asked for an update. He informed us they were still under attack from the south.

We told him we were two minutes out and would begin our attack over their compound.

The United States Army supplied the Vietnamese Army with ammunition, basic field supplies, and food, but the most important aid we gave them was air support. There was no Vietnamese Air Force! There had been some old World War II propeller-driven planes when America first arrived but they had long outlived their usefulness. The expense was too great to supply South Vietnam with modern aircraft.

We could see the red tracers of automatic weapon fire as we started our first run; we launched two rockets and a burst of machine gun fire. The rockets flashed bright in the night sky as they rushed toward their target. Their white phosphorus war heads exploded in a burst that reminded me of hundreds of 4th of July sparklers.

These sparklers don't burn out in pretty bright colors; they melt, fiercely, deep into your skin and won't stop burning until the phosphorous burns through the body, or runs out of oxygen.

As we broke contact, our wingman opened fire to protect our turn. His rockets burst below us, lighting up the night sky as we turned away from the fighting. The enemy could not see us but fired into the air where they believed we were.

As we entered our third run, my commander called for backup, as our ammunition was running low. The "five-minute" alert team was already in their aircraft monitoring the battle. They immediately began startup, and were on station within five minutes.

The ARVN advisor radioed that the enemy had broken contact and a medevac was needed. Our medevac had been on station about five miles out, waiting for clearance to land.

Our backup fire team continued to fire at the enemy, who had retreated into a nearby gulch and was rapidly leaving the area.

We contacted the medevac and he began his approach to the now-lit compound. We fell in behind to protect his landing.

Both fire teams stayed on station until he pulled power and took the wounded to medical aide. The ARVN advisor, a U.S. Army captain, radioed us and told us, "The camp commander sends his thanks; your quick response saved many lives and has driven the enemy away. Thank you for your assistance. You are free to return to your base." It was nearly two hours since we had left base camp.

We were told later their base commander had put us in for the "Vietnamese Cross of Gallantry," their nation's highest award.

Later, I completely forgot the battle and being put in for the award.

After leaving the military, I was looking up the ribbons that had been placed on my uniform at Fort Wolters, my after-Vietnam post. I was surprised to find I had received two of those awards – one for that battle and one awarded to the 11th as a unit.

I was learning every time I left the ground, and each mission brought me closer to my own command.

One by one, the pilots that had been there when I arrived were rotating home. I was still a junior pilot without my own call sign, but no longer the new guy.

My flying time increased each month: 70 hours in May, as the rains started, June increased to 72, and July, 79. The rain also increased in quantity and duration.

One day a small cloud appeared, but was gone in a short time. Every day, about the same time, the clouds arrived. Each time they were bigger and bigger, until one day they stayed, and the sky fell. It rained so hard I couldn't see my hand in front of my face! I tried it, and I couldn't!

Rain also brings out another life form – huge red spiders! They are everywhere. They come out of the ground, from under bushes and tents, and they disappear just as fast when the rain stops.

Everything was wet – really wet! The red dirt was now red mud, and it stuck to everything. It was very difficult to get off my boots and out of my clothes.

We were not aware at the time, but the Air Force was running a secret rain seeding mission. They were dropping silver iodide into the monsoon clouds during 1967 and 1968. Rain seeding caused the monsoons to be more intense and last longer. It was intended to delay or stop enemy movement and resupply. Unfortunately, it also made our flying much more difficult and dangerous.

August saw my flight time reach 88 hours, including my first weather-related instrument time. I remembered my instrument training at Fort Wolters; it had not been my greatest moment.

In Vietnam, though, it was a matter of survival. We were flying a daytime mission, making our way home, when the weather closed in around us. The winds started whipping, rain pelted our windshield, and our crew quickly closed their side doors to avoid getting soaked. Our wingman moved in closer and higher above us, so he could see our lights and follow our lead. We stayed on our compass heading and cleared the storm clouds 20 minutes later. That wasn't so bad! I watched the gauges for my commander; I didn't even break a sweat!

Rank is everything in the military; it's so important that they track it by hours, minutes, and alphabetical order. There are only two things that foul up that order: one is promotion and the other is air craft command. Believe it or not, the latter outranks the former.

My friend Rob was the 1st Infantry commander's pilot. On the ground, he followed the general's orders. In the air, he outranked the general.

On one occasion, the general ordered Rob to fly low and slow over an ongoing battle. Rob informed the general it was too dangerous and he couldn't follow that order. Returning to the ground, the general requested a new pilot. His crew requested to continue to fly with Rob.

Over the radio, rank is identified by call sign. In Air Cav, under normal circumstances, the first number designates your platoon, the second tells your position in the platoon. 1-1 would normally mean 1st Platoon, leader of 1st Squad, and so on. There are 4 squads; 1-1 to 1-4 would be squad leaders, usually lieutenants. 1-6 would be the platoon leader, usually a major, and 1-5 the executive officer, second in command, also a major or a captain.

As a warrant officer, I would normally never have a command position, or number. But this was war; there was nothing normal about it.

As August slipped away, the last of the senior pilots prepared to leave. One morning our company commander called me into his office. He reminded me we were losing "Thunderhorse 25," 2nd Platoon's elder statesman. He looked me in the eye and asked, "You're up next. Are you ready for this?"

"Yes, Sir!" I replied.

On September 5, 1967, I became "Thunderhorse 25"; I was an aircraft commander. The only one outranking me in the air was my fire team leader. The men on the ground thought I was a major.

Army Helicopter number 522 was now my responsibility. 522 came equipped with 14 rockets and four M60 machine guns mounted on its side. It also had 2 M60s, one each for my door gunner and crew chief.

A few months later, we equipped 522 with the unit's first mini guns. Mini guns are five-barrel machine guns that spin as they fire. I could fire a lot of rounds in a very short time. I was the second ship in the fire team, at least for another month, but I officially had my first command.

CHAPTER NINE
FLYING WINGMAN (VIETNAM PART 4)

Between Blackhorse Base Camp and Vung Tau, not far from the Michelin Rubber Plantation, was an area called "No Man's Land/ Free-Fire Zone."

Part of Operation Kittyhawk was disruption of the North Vietnamese Army and Vietcong plans for mass attacks. In order to disrupt, it was necessary to locate the enemy, their headquarters, and ammo dumps. This "No Man's Land" was a known Vietcong hangout. The problem was, it was large, dense, and had no visible trails.

"No Man's Land" means just what it says – no one is allowed in the restricted area. It had no development, farm, or town, only scrub trees as far as the eye could see, occasionally broken by a tree or two that topped out at 50 or 60 feet.

Up until this new designation, it had been the domain of woodcutters and an occasional hunter trying to feed his family. The locals were well aware of the enemy's movements, and had been warned to stay clear.

When we were sent to patrol the area, it became a "Free-Fire Zone." Anything we saw, we were cleared to kill or destroy, even animals if the fire team leader deemed them an enemy asset.

In the grasslands were herds of water buffalo. The VC would run their tame animals among the herds during the day and recover them at dusk. They used these animals in place of trucks to carry large loads. The herds seldom wandered into heavily-treed areas; they were just too large to navigate the tightly-knit brush and trees.

About an hour into our patrol, we spotted a thatched hut, hidden among the taller trees. It was miles from any road and seemed unlikely to be a hunter's cabin. There was no movement around or near the hut; a small stream meandered through the trees.

The radio crackled and the voice of my fire team leader said, "Doug, go ahead and put a rocket into that hooch. It's definitely in 'No Man's Land!' Go ahead and destroy it!"

I swung my craft around and lined up a rocket attack. Our mission was to ensure the enemy had nothing usable in the area, and, if nothing else, I would get some great target practice. My first rocket hit flat against the ground, bounced through the door, and hit the back wall. It exploded in a white phosphorous fireball. We circled the flaming hut to be sure of its destruction.

Seeing the hut fully involved, my fire team leader turned towards home. We were about a quarter-mile away when there was a tremendous explosion.

Turning back, we observed a huge fireball and mushroom cloud. There must have been a large stockpile of munitions hidden under the hut's false floor.

Explosion after explosion threw sparks and expended shells into the nearby brush. This had been a major ammo dump. The wet weather kept the fire from spreading into the smaller trees and bush; it could have been a real wildfire. I like to believe we saved lives that day; at least we disrupted the VC activities and put a crimp in their plans.

Living in Oregon, God has blessed us with beautiful mountains and gorgeous hiking trails. Through the years, we've heard tales of individuals getting lost, injured, or dying trying to enjoy these blessings.

One thing most of these tragedies had in common – the victims were not fully prepared! Weather can change within minutes. The forests are dense and full of hazards. Not just bears, mountain lions, and angry deer – there are large canyons, streams, and gullies hidden among the trees. Slippery trails lead to falls for the unwary. It's always raining somewhere in Oregon!

Being prepared means "not going alone!" It is important to carry location devices, supplies, and enough fresh water to get you safely through your trip.

Our long-range reconnaissance patrols (LRRP) were prepared for everything.

We couldn't fly as far or as often during the heaviest monsoons. Emergencies were the exception.

One of our long-range recon patrols had been ambushed and was desperately calling for help. These patrols consist of six to eight men. They pack all their supplies and ammo, and are dropped into the jungle, delta, or mountains. They are on patrol for three to 10 days, sometimes longer, with nothing but a radio for communication. Their job is to find heavy-use areas and set up observation posts. They would radio their position and alert headquarters if they spotted enemy movements.

Headquarters would use the information to decide where to place our tank units to the best advantage.

I was flying second ship on "30-second" alert team, when the alarm sounded. The heavy rain hadn't started. It was early afternoon, so we headed straight to their position, followed by two slicks, UH-1 D models, who would pull the team out.

When we arrived, they were still desperately calling for help: "We're surrounded and taking fire. We're pinned down in a stand of tall trees. We need help now!"

The fire team leader radioed back, "We're here! Throw smoke and we'll identify." Throwing smoke meant to throw out a smoke grenade. The military had provided its men with a series of colored smoke canisters. When they needed assistance, they pulled the pin on a canister and the smoke guided aid to their location.

The VC had learned this tactic and had captured or been supplied with smoke canisters from the Chinese. They would throw their own canisters to confuse and ambush our rescue effort.

As the smoke filtered through the treetops, my fire team leader radioed to the LRRP team, "I identify yellow smoke!" The LRRP team leader responded, "Yes, yellow smoke. They're all around us."

We laid down suppressing fire until they felt secure enough for pickup. The trees were tall and dense; we couldn't see them, or the enemy, and had to rely on their radio to tell us where, and if, to shoot.

The first slick hovered above their position and let out two recovery lines.

The first two men grabbed the ropes and anchored on. The slick flew them several miles, dangling from the ropes, to where a tank unit had established a field outpost.

The next slick hovered into position. Panic set in as all four remaining men, believing the enemy was returning, grabbed the two lines! Because of the extra weight and hot humid weather, the aircraft started settling into the trees.

The pilot was forced to nose the craft forward, dragging the four men through the trees and knocking one off a line. The other was unconscious and dangling from the same line. The two young soldiers on the other line had not hit the tree trunk, but were scraped and battered by the surrounding tree limbs. The slick pilot radioed ahead, "I have three injured men on my recovery lines. Will need medical assistance."

He brought the aircraft to a hover above the circle of tanks and A-CAVs. The medics, assisted by several tank crew members, released the injured soldiers from their rescue lines and began medical treatment. The slick landed in the same area in case they were needed to evacuate any of the injured troops.

The first slick who had just returned, hovered over the spot trying to make contact with the lost man.

The clouds were getting darker; although it was still mid-afternoon, we were rapidly losing our light. Within minutes the monsoon broke loose! We could see nothing! The slick with the wounded soldiers had stayed with the tank unit. We were not so fortunate. Our fire team was at a higher altitude and the rain took visibility to practically nothing.

As wingman, I was flying even higher than the lead craft. The last thing I saw was a large hill in front of me. I told my leader I was going to climb out of the storm.

I called our local radar and asked for a vector out of the storm. They told me to "squawk my parrot." My parrot was the emergency transmitter attached to our radio. I pushed the red button and waited for his response. He had me push the button three times, but because of the lightning, he could not get a fix on my position. He told me to climb to 39,000 feet on a heading of 280 feet. I responded, "I'm a U.S. Army helicopter." He replied, "Good luck. There's no way I can help you!"

I looked around my aircraft. The suddenness of the downpour and the bright flashes of our navigation lights had caused my crew to experience vertigo! I cannot tell you, unless you have experienced vertigo, how strange you feel. I couldn't get my eyes to focus on my instruments; I did not know what was up or what was down.

I tried to concentrate, but my mind was swimming; I didn't know what to do.

At that moment, the Lord put his hands on mine and eased me down out of the heavy downpour. We ended up behind and off to the side of the lead aircraft. Thank you, Lord!

I have no other way to explain it. Our God is an awesome God. He is in control!

My vertigo cleared as my mind found something to focus on. I could see the treetops below me. I should have looked at my instruments as I did when I was the co-pilot in other bad weather situations. I glanced at my crew. They were all moving and trying to focus.

I later talked with my crew about what they had seen and felt. My co-pilot, a young man who had arrived in country a few weeks earlier, said, "I had no idea what was happening. I felt like I was floating and I didn't know which way was up or down." The other crew members both echoed his statement and the crew chief added, "I just held onto my door gun and tried not to vomit."

Ours was not the only miracle that occurred that night; the second slick had also been caught in the storm. When the lost soldier did not respond, the slick pilot ordered the crew to pull their ropes and then climbed to a safer altitude.

When the storm broke, he was much higher than I had been, and was flying alone. He had immediately gone on instruments, and he and his pilot had avoided vertigo.

They had also attempted to contact radar for help. The storm was electrical, heavy lightning, strong winds, and no way for radar to find them. He had decided to climb, not knowing the clouds were topped at 38,000 feet. Helicopters have no oxygen, but they were committed.

They climbed to 2,500 feet and picked a course they believed would bring them to safety. After flying for over two hours and with fuel running low, they decided to turn around and descend. They had been flying towards the ocean and were unsure of their current position.

They had five minutes of fuel left when they broke free of the clouds and saw a sandy beach in front of them; they set down on the beach facing inland. They had been flying out over the South China Sea for almost half an hour.

A South Vietnamese patrol with an American advisor had heard the helicopter descending, found the ship, and protected it. A supply ship came with fuel the next morning. Not the best way to have a trip to the beach. I wonder if they even heard the gentle breaking of the waves that cold, dark night.

The next morning, an 11th Armor tank patrol made it to the original recovery area and found the lost man. He was unconscious with several broken bones, but survived.

Our fire team was able to contact a tank platoon patrolling the nearby area, and they guided us to their bivouac. We spent the night surrounded by tanks and A-CAVs – not a five-star sleeping accommodation, but boy did I feel safe.

Not everything had a happy ending. A group from Saigon had finished their business at Blackhorse Base Camp and was anxious to get home. The pilots had been warned that a monsoon was rapidly moving in from the South China Sea and it would be a dangerous flight. They felt since their journey was only 40 miles, they could make it before the heavy storm started. They didn't.

The storm broke minutes after they left Blackhorse. The pilot, in his attempt to get away from the torrential downpour, either tried to turn back or fly around the storm and lost control, as I had done, and flew into the surrounding jungle. Everyone in the aircraft died in the ensuing crash. It was months before the crash sight was located and the bodies recovered.

Flying wing had some very interesting moments. On a mission north of Saigon, we were sent to patrol the central lowlands. The French had built a huge power line that stretched from Saigon, north. It had six to eight very thick lines that were strung between tall, steel towers. The towers were spaced 100 to 150 yards apart.

Beautiful farmland stretched as far as the eye could see. Small streams fed the area from the hills surrounding the lowlands. The sad thing was, there were no people. No farmhouses, just bare, untended land. The enemy had destroyed every sign of life.

There were the power lines, of course, but no power ran through them. They had been cut long before I arrived in country.

In flight school, we had been taught to stay clear of power lines, since you couldn't always see every line. If you had to cross them, you flew over the poles or towers.

We had seen some interesting movement along the towers. The trees, brush, and jungle vines had encroached and were beginning to climb and cover the unattended structures. Most of the movement ended up being the wind blowing or animals – monkeys, deer, or wild pigs.

Something had caught my fire team leader's attention and he had taken his aircraft much too close to the power lines.

I had taken a position about 200 yards behind him so I could observe the whole area while he was taking a closer look. The power lines suddenly took a sharp right turn and he was heading right for them.

When he failed to turn, I radioed him to inform him of the imminent danger. Too late! He had flown right into the center of the lines.

As we watched, fearing the worst, his craft made several unusual dips and turns. It went nose down then immediately up, right, left, and then down again. We watched in amazement as he came out the other side of the enormous lines.

In a very excited voice I asked him, "Did you just fly THROUGH those lines?" He was very slow in replying, but insisted over and over, "NO! NO! NO! I didn't!"

The lines had been so damaged some were hanging halfway to the ground, while others were still tight.

I flew over the nearest tower to rejoin him, and passed by where he had flown. My crew was still jabbering, "Mr. Eggerth, did he really fly through those wires? A helicopter can't do that!" The other replied, "Yes! He did! I saw it. That was amazing!" They had seen exactly what I saw.

He told me later that he had gotten distracted by something on the ground, and lost sight of the lines. He swore again and again he had gone UNDER the lines and not through them.

His crew, all three of them, said they had no idea what happened. Their eyes had all been closed as their lives had passed before them.

One of my last missions as a wingman has long stuck in my mind. I was now a senior pilot and often flew as fire team leader. The captain had me fly wing for a senior pilot who had just transferred from flying slicks. He had no experience as a gunship pilot and had never had a wingman.

We had been assigned to cover A Troop during a search-and-destroy mission in the Delta.

The Mekong River meanders from its source in Laos through Cambodia, until it spreads its waters into the southern tip of Vietnam and out into the South China Sea.

The spreading of the river, known as the Delta, has long been a source of great joy, and pain, for thousands of years. There is enough rice grown in the Delta to feed the entire population of China for any number of years.

Throughout the centuries, many nations have coveted that rice, including China at that time. With the support of China, the North Vietnamese were making an all-out effort to gain that rice, and all of South Vietnam. China would gain a great foothold in the area if they were successful.

We were stationed somewhere around Can Tho, in the northern Delta. There was a small airfield where we were bivouacked.

I had a natural sense of direction and above-average hand-eye coordination. I was also stubborn – just ask my brother! These traits help when flying a gunship, and leading a fire team.

It was late evening and our troop had settled in for the night. We weren't expecting any more action. The airfield was an hour flight from Blackhorse, so they had sent two fire teams.

The troop had set up a radio near our bunks so we could monitor any local action. If the troop needed us, we could be ready within minutes.

We were on call that night, so when we heard the six-man LRRP team call for help, we grabbed our gear and raced to our choppers. We had been aware of their location, so we knew what direction to head. They were patrolling deep in the Delta, a 45-minute flight from our bivouac.

It was completely dark when we arrived. Dark in the Mekong Delta is not bad in the moonlight. There is more water than solid ground and it is easy to tell the difference. The moon's silver light reflects off the water with a bright mirrored shine. The mirrors are bordered by the many dirt dikes that separate each family's rice paddy. The dikes are wide enough to accommodate trails or small roads. Each corner is large enough for a family to set up their living space during planting and harvest seasons.

The only problem was, there was no moon!

We knew approximately where the team was, but it was too dark to see. We asked the team leader to help us identify their location. They placed a small strobe light in the middle of the team; it could only be seen from the air. From 500 feet we could easily see the small strobe flashing in the darkness.

The team leader's voice was high pitched with fear as he called out, "They're all around us! We have no cover. They're all around us." They feared they would be overrun at any moment.

My rookie fire team leader laid down gunfire farther out from their position. They radioed, "You're too far out. You've got to shoot closer." I cut the distance in half, but they still said, "Closer." Again I cut the distance, and again, "Closer!" My next pass I closed my eyes and shot right over the top of them. I just knew they were all dead! An excited voice yelled over the radio, "You got them. They're running. You got them."

We stayed long enough to ensure that all the LRRP team were uninjured and felt safe, and then we headed home.

Our fire team leader, the slick pilot, was not used to long-distance navigation, especially at night. I knew right away something was wrong. My compass told me we were heading the wrong way. I turned on my navigational aid and it also showed us flying the wrong direction.

I radioed him with my concern, but he refused to believe me. He radioed back, "We're headed correctly. My instrument says I'm right on track!" Where had I heard this before? After a few more minutes rechecking my navigational aids, I told him, "I am not going to continue flying this direction. We're heading the wrong way, deeper into the Delta. If you don't turn back soon, we won't have enough fuel to make it home."

Reluctantly, he finally turned 180 degrees and corrected his error. Half an hour later, my 20-minute warning light came on.

Bell Helicopter guarantees its helicopter engine will have enough fuel to keep running for at least 20 minutes when the warning light comes on. 38 minutes later, our leader was lining up for a normal approach to our small, now brightly-lit airfield.

I told him, "Look out!" and went screaming past him, ready to make an engine failure landing. I needed enough airspeed to make the runway so I could slide in if the engine failed.

The engine never quit! I hovered to a landing with 45 minutes on the clock, 25 minutes past the guaranteed warning light time. Again, thank you, Lord!

One late night, around 1:00 or 2:00 a.m., our fire team was returning from an extended mission with one of our Cav units. We had been stationed at a lonely outpost with a small airfield and concrete blockhouses.

We had finished fueling and rearming both aircraft, and the eight of us had picked up our gear and were heading for bed.

It was a dark, moonless night; the beautiful array of stars that spread across the black-velvet sky emitted no usable light. Our military flashlights provided our only aid as we made our way to the gray, concrete buildings.

Suddenly the night turned to broad daylight!

At first I thought it was an aerial flare, but there were no shadows. When a flare is launched into the air, it rushes from its launch tube and ignites. It also deploys its attached parachute. As the flare returns to the ground, it swings back and forth, and floats with the wind. The flare produces strange shadows that move with its swinging and descending motion.

Our crew stared up at the shining bright light in awe! I looked around me and the buildings were lit like midday. I could see the horizon! The nearby trees caught the light; their limbs stood out and threw midday shadows on their neighbors. I looked at the ground where I stood; to my amazement I saw no shadow.

Just as suddenly as it was there, it was gone. There had been no sound, no aircraft noise, and no sizzle of a falling flare. We stood there stunned! The bright light had made us night blind; it was several minutes before our flashlights provided enough visibility for us to move.

We included our strange sighting in our after-action report. Days later our fire team was reminded of our security clearance and told, "You saw nothing!"

It's been 50 years and I still have no idea what we saw!

Chapter Ten
My Own Fire Team, Cats, and Cherry Bars (Vietnam Part 5)

I was assigned to take my fire team from somewhere near Tay Ninh to patrol along the Cambodian border. My mission was to look for any movement coming out of Cambodia or off the Ho Chi Minh Trail.

The Trail was the main route the North Vietnamese used to infiltrate South Vietnam. Their troops and supplies were smuggled through Laos and Cambodia across mountains, through canyons, dense forests, and jungles.

It was late November or early December, and it was dry. The area we flew over was a combination of brown elephant grass and scrub trees. The closer we got to the Cambodian border, the thicker the trees.

Intelligence had told us there was activity coming down the trail. The 11th was tasked with determining what kind of activity it was and how much, and if possible, to make contact. We weren't aware at the time, but the largest North Vietnamese attack of the war—the Tet Offensive—was mere months away. My fire team was to scout ahead of the tanks' advances.

I was following a number of trails that wandered back and forth among the smaller scrub trees, when we suddenly spotted a bicycle messenger crossing the border.

We were 40 miles from any village or military outpost; this must be an enemy courier. I turned and headed directly at him; he was just coming past a clump of tall elephant grass and had not seen or heard us coming. When he saw my helicopter, he jumped off his bike and dived into the brush.

I fired a rocket at the last place I had seen him; it exploded in a burst of white phosphorous spray. We continued circling and firing into the area, but could not locate him or his body. We shot up his bicycle, still lying on the trail. If he survived, he was going to have to walk.

A small fire was burning in the scrub brush where my rocket had exploded. With fuel running low, I headed my team back to base camp.

The next morning, my commanding officer informed me my rocket had started a major brush fire, and it was spreading rapidly. He told me to take my fire team and continue scanning the area, and keep an eye on the fire.

I took my team back towards the border. Flying east, we quickly spotted the now-billowing smoke. The grassland fire had engulfed several acres and was spreading towards the Cambodian jungle.

I led my team ahead of the fire and renewed the search for enemy forces. We again circled the area with no luck. We headed back towards the fire. As I was flying over a tall tree, it exploded under my aircraft and pushed us 200 feet higher.

The exhilarating feeling of going from 40 feet to 200 in half a second can only be described as riding the downside of a rollercoaster but going up, it was totally unexpected!

Apparently the fire had been burning around the base and had heated the watery core. As the temperature rose, the pressure caused the tree to explode upward in a sudden burst of steam.

The fire continued into the jungle and burnt itself out in the watery green foliage. We made no further contact with the enemy on that mission. The fire may have forced the enemy further into the dense Cambodian jungle.

I am and always have been a "cat lover!" I grew up in an ugly, old rectangular wooden house my grandfather built by hand in the late 1890s. An ancient furnace was under the floor and came up directly into the center of the house.

He had placed a metal furnace screen over the opening to keep my grandma from falling in. My younger brother and I would sit on the screen in our pajamas and try to get warm. The problem with this scenario was our cat. He was a big, tough tomcat, and he ruled the house, the yard, and the neighborhood. That furnace grate was his favorite spot and he did not take it kindly when we encroached on his territory.

Our home had a small front porch with a wide ledge that ran along two sides. Junior, the cat, sat on the front ledge to get the sun, and keep an eye on his domain. I often lay on the other ledge for similar reasons.

Once, a large boxer came trotting across the street, heading for Junior's protectorate. I knew trouble was brewing! I watched as Junior's eye opened, his fir bristled, and his body tensed. He waited until the first paw touched his side of the street, and he was off in a flash.

The last I saw of the boxer, he was fleeing back where he had come, with a very large and annoyed cat attached to his back. Five minutes later, Junior returned, stretched, cleaned his paws, and went back to his peaceful nap.

My cat was the epitome of patience, stubbornness, awareness, watchfulness, and unwavering commitment, all things I worked at while performing my duties in the military.

I knew my aircraft. I knew every sound it made, how it should feel in a turn, and how much power it could give me on demand. 522 had become as much a part of me as any of my other body parts. My crew chief, door gunner, and 522 were my family. I needed them and they needed me.

The maintenance officer and I had been going head to head over a severe vibration in 522's rotor. He had stripped my gunship, flown it around, and found no vibration. After replacing my guns, he yelled at me and said, "There's nothing wrong!"

But I knew what I had felt and heard; I also had the backing of my crew, who had experienced the same vibration. I pulled 522 out of the maintenance area and flew out to the practice range. I pushed the cyclic forward, went into a power dive, and shot off a rocket.

As I pulled out of the dive, the rotor started shaking. The more power I applied the stronger the vibration. My crew held on tight, with eyes closed, as the powerful helicopter tried to shake itself apart. I leveled out and the vibration slowly subsided.

I flew directly back to the maintenance area and stormed into the office. I tossed my log book on his desk and said, "I'm 'red X-ing' 522."

When a pilot puts a red "X" in his log book, the aircraft cannot be flown again until maintenance fixes the problem.

He glared at me and said, "What now!" I told him what happened and he called his crew chief in and told him to replace the rotor blade. He added, "Since it's going to be a few days to get a new rotor, we'll do 522's routine maintenance a little early."

Three days later I was called to the maintenance office. The officer was still irritated, but informed me they had finished the routine inspection and a new rotor was now attached to 522.

In a parting shot he said, "I've sent the old rotor to Saigon to get x-rayed, and we'll see if anything is REALLY wrong."

As I left headquarters to recover 522, I had been given an assignment by my commanding officer. I called my crew, and told my wingman we had a mission. We were to be airborne as soon as I pulled 522 from maintenance.

We were departing Blackhorse when suddenly there was a change in engine sound and a loud "pop!" I quickly scanned my instruments and looked back at my crew. My co-pilot, who had just arrived in country, yelled "What's wrong? What's wrong?" The crew was looking into the engine compartment for any visible problems.

Just then my wingman radioed, "There's fireballs coming from your engine."

I called Blackhorse tower, declared an emergency, and quickly swung back to the runway. I set down in maintenance, again! The maintenance fire team came running out with fire extinguishers. After shutting down, the fire stopped spitting from the engine cowl and went out.

The maintenance crew removed the cowl and inspected the engine compartment.

Three hours later, they had me pick up my aircraft. The maintenance officer apologized; a new worker had been assigned to grease the engine and had wiped globs of grease off his hands onto the engine intake. The grease globs exploded in fireballs as they passed through the red-hot turbines.

A week later, the maintenance officer called to tell me the x-ray report was back. It showed a wide crack, running the length of the blade. He apologized and said, "It was a good thing you grounded 522. The blade could have broken apart at any time."

When he removed the guns and equipment, he had also removed the extra weight that was stressing the rotor blade.

My team had been alert to anything out of the ordinary, just like my cat, and it proved to be a lifesaver – "All things work together for good to those who love the Lord!" He sent my cat, Junior, to teach me valuable life lessons when I was only seven years old. Praise the Lord for his goodness and mercy!

Around this time, we lost our commanding officer. He was wounded in action and replaced by Colonel George Patton Junior, son of World War II's General Patton. He was a fine officer, dedicated to tanks and helicopters. He learned to fly upon his return to the States.

A normal fire team consisted of two aircraft, but when we received special orders, we flew in three-craft teams. This was very rare and meant Central Command felt something big was in the air.

We were again flying near the Cambodian border. Our platoon leader took the lead of the three-craft team.

One of our long-range recon patrols had spotted a large number of enemy moving around the border. Saigon was concerned by the reports and sent the 11th to make contact, disrupt, and hopefully destroy those troops.

Trying to keep our presence as quiet as possible, we were treetop level. Flying low and fast kept the sound of our engines and rotors behind us as the trees helped dampen the sound.

Our leader dropped into an open area, full of large clumps of elephant grass. He ran head on into a battalion of North Vietnamese regulars trying to navigate the six-foot-tall, razor-sharp grass.

We were told to split up and pick our targets. Over the next half hour, we raised havoc on the enemy. Between the elephant grass and flying lead, the enemy didn't know which way to turn, and it was a mad dash in every direction.

There were so many targets, I almost forgot to look to see where I was going. I pulled my eyes off my target and looked up just in time to see one of our helicopters coming straight at me. I veered right, just as he did, and we continued our attack.

The intelligence had paid off big time. There were 300 enemy soldiers caught in the open that day. Very few made it back into the protection of the scrub trees.

When we arrived back at Blackhorse, I was told to take my team to the quartermaster's and pick up new helmets. The military brass back home decided we needed bulletproof helmets. The idea wasn't so bad, but the added weight gave me headaches. I complained I couldn't function with a continual headache. I was told there was nothing they could do; I had to wear the heavy pain maker.

I sat in my tent looking at both helmets; there were two differences in their design. The new one was much heavier and the mouth piece speaker had a different design.

The old mouth piece was made of solid grey plastic that swiveled where it attached to the helmet. The new mouth piece was between a pair of chrome wires that attached to the helmet in the same way. The wires had two swivels and had a distinctly different look.

I switched the mouth pieces with little effort and no one seemed to notice. The headaches were gone and I finished the tour with my redesigned old helmet.

One morning patrol, south of Blackhorse, I was flying about 50 feet above the jungle. There had been very little rain, but the jungle was still dark green and full of life. Suddenly an enormous flock of parakeets rose out of the trees and encircled both helicopters.

One minute it was bright sunshine, the next it was like a multicolored cloud had blocked the sun, and it was beautiful! There must have been a million birds, every color of the rainbow, in that enormous flock.

They circled us several times, swooping, swirling, and moving like a multicolored wave. Just as suddenly as they appeared, they disappeared back into the jungle foliage! What an awesome display of God's majesty!

Napoleon is believed to have said, "An Army marches on its stomach!" But it could just as easily have been any private in any army.

Food, lots of it. It's even better if it comes from someone you love. My beautiful bride-to-be sent me box after box of chocolate chip cookies and maraschino cherry bars. These were the best chocolate chip cookies ever made: homemade, beautifully browned, soft, and chewy.

I don't know how she did it, but they smelled and tasted like they just came out of her hot oven. And they were all mine. Well, that's what I thought at first!

Don't mention this to her, but I'm not much of a cherry bar kind-of-guy. I'd eat them, maybe, but they are not my favorite.

I made a deal with my roommates: "You get the bars. I get ALL the chocolate chip cookies."

I laid the bars on the table and they each took one. I think the whole batch lasted 10 or 15 seconds. When I saw the look on their faces, I knew I had to quickly hide my cookies. They couldn't wait for my next box to arrive. The chocolate chip cookies, though, were mine, ALL MINE!

I never mentioned this to my new bride until long after I returned from Vietnam. Once, she made some cherry bars for Christmas and offered me one. I told her, "No thanks!" She looked at me funny and said, "What about the ones I sent you in Vietnam?" I *carefully* explained what I had done.

"When they saw a box come for me, they all started salivating. It was a matter of life and death; you saved my life and made my roommates so happy, sending us a taste of home. What a wonderful, refreshing, and uplifting thing you did."

She looked back at me with a skeptical squint. "You better not tell Jill and Lori (her two young nieces). I wouldn't let them eat but one. I told them, 'These are for Doug!'"

At Christmas time, I received three boxed Christmas trees, one each from my wife's aunt and uncle, my folks and fiancée, and one from the church.

I gave one to my crew, and one to each of the 2nd Platoon officers' tents. It was a very merry Christmas; they were all thrilled to get their own shiny, green, plastic, colorfully-lit tree. We didn't get to enjoy them for long, though; we were called to Lai Khe for a special mission.

The next morning, all three fire teams left for our temporary assignment at 1st Infantry's local headquarters. Things had been quiet at Blackhorse and my friend Rob said, "Lai Khe is quiet as a mouse." When we arrived, tents had been erected in the rubber trees, so we settled in for the night.

I was just sitting down on my green Army cot, when there were several explosions and gunfire. Our captain called us to his tent. "Spread around camp," he said. "Go!"

My two crewmen and I were sent to one corner of the camp and told, "Hold your ground. Command believes we're about to be overrun."

I had a grenade and my .45 Automatic with seven rounds. My crew had M16 field rifles with one clip each.

We placed a Claymore mine out in front of us, lay on the ground behind two rubber trees, and waited!

We'd been lying there for 10 minutes, when the kid to my right said, "Mr. Eggerth, I think I heard something!" I responded, "No you didn't!" I was ready to fight, but very glad when moments later we were called back to our tents. The enemy had thrown two grenades, fired a few rounds, and ran off.

A few days later, on December 22, 1967, our main mission arrived: Bob Hope!

Our fire teams were assigned to fly cover as Bob Hope and his entertainment troop entertained the 1st Infantry troops.

My team was primary; I was to protect his landing, then stay on station as long as he was on the ground. The backup teams were to be ready if an attack happened or I was running low on fuel.

His pilot informed me he was 10 minutes out. I made sure there was no activity in his path, notified the tower it was clear, and fell in behind to cover his approach. When I was sure the aircraft was safely on the ground, I assumed my assigned station circling the compound.

We did get to watch the show, from 500 feet, as we flew round and round the base camp for two hours, dodging aircraft from several other units.

When the show ended, there was no sticking around. We watched as the aircraft taxied to the end of the runway. We lost sight of them moments after takeoff. I am very happy to say there was no excitement during my watch, except on stage!

50 years later, my friend Rob informed me he had spent the whole show sitting in the 7th row with the senior officers. He also added, "Raquel Welch was very beautiful." Thanks, Rob!

The 1st Infantry was not the only unit our fire teams were farmed out to. I was often sent to Bearcat Base Camp to aid the 9th Infantry Division. Bearcat was east of Blackhorse on Hwy 15 between Bien Hoa and Vung Tau.

The 9th had arrived in Vietnam in January 1967, and moved into Bearcat. The 1st Battalion, 11th Artillery established its firebase there the same time. I had to call Bearcat for artillery clearance whenever I flew near Bien Hoa or Saigon.

We slept in or under our aircraft the whole time we were attached to the 9th.

One afternoon I was hovering in for a landing. I had to fly over the artillery in order to reach my landing spot. Just as I moved past the gun, there was an enormous explosion. They had fired a round right over my tail.

That evening we heard another explosion. It didn't sound like the last, so I jumped up to see what had happened. There were several A-CAVs parked nearby and one was under repair. A-CAVs are made of magnesium, which burns hot and long.

The crew needed to remove the engine, but forgot to remove the battery. As they pulled the engine, the battery sparked and the magnesium began to burn.

You cannot put magnesium out. Underwater flares are made of magnesium. There is nothing you can put on or over it that will put it out.

It burned all that night and most of the next day. We sat in our aircraft and watched the sparks jump in a multicolored display.

When the vehicle finally burned itself out, there was nothing but a pile of ash, and the smell of burnt rubber.

My old crew rotated home the same day my new crew chief rotated in. I found him highly experienced and quick to learn the ways of 522.

My new door gunner was an 18-year-old youngster who had been trained as a cook's assistant. When he arrived at Blackhorse, my old door gunner had just left.

Since the young soldier had been cross-trained on the M60 machine gun and the need for a door gunner was greater than for a cook's assistant, he was sent to see me.

I assembled my fire team and introduced our new gunner to them and 522. He smiled when he saw his new M60. I took the team to our practice area and had him demonstrate his skills. Much to our satisfaction, he proved he was more capable with an M60 than any potato peeler. He stayed with me until I left for home.

Late January 1968, we were just south of Blackhorse at a huge rubber plantation owned by the Michelin Corporation. We were covering A Troop as they patrolled with their A-CAVs and tanks. They had taken some fire but no major contact. We were asked to fly the perimeter and report any movement.

As we flew over the sprawling acres of rubber trees, we came to the main house. Not only did they have perfectly manicured grounds, but a beautiful swimming pool, all nestled on top of a small hill.

They were a French family with two teenage daughters, who happened to be sunbathing poolside. My crew requested multiple flyovers to ensure they were safe.

Years after I left the military, I was at Maclaren Youth Correctional Facility, working an evening shift. The cottage assistant manager and I were talking about Vietnam and I was relating this story. Mike got wide-eyed and asked what unit I was with. I told him Air Cav Troop, 11th Armored Cavalry. He jumped up and said, "You were talking to me." Turns out he was the medic and radio man of that very A Troop unit, on that very mission.

He asked my call sign. When I told him I was Thunderhorse 25, he exclaimed, "I use to talk to you all the time. It's a very small world!"

Everything was fairly quiet around the plantation; there had been no further contact with the enemy. We weren't sure why, but a few days later our headquarters added B and C Troops to expand our search area.

Air Cav Troop continued to fly out of Blackhorse in support of our ground units. The majority of the 11th was around the plantation, but squads from each unit were still carrying out patrols for our other assignments.

My fire team was up north, with a unit clearing highways near Bien Hoa. We had other fire teams working south and around the plantation. Air Cav, 1st Platoon, was still on alert at base camp.

We had not been able to make contact with the enemy for several weeks. Every mission had been peaceful and quiet.

On January 28, 1968 during a recon and road clearing operation, the Cav unit I was protecting came under heavy fire and called for assistance. The captain had the lead that day, and was breaking in a new pilot, so he had me flying wing. When we arrived on station, we were informed the enemy had taken over a small village and ambushed the ground unit as they passed by.

There was a large rubber curing plant in the center of the village that provided their main source of income. These curing plants received the raw rubber from the many rubber plantations in the area. They cured the raw rubber in large vats, before sending it to other countries for processing.

The enemy had fortified the plant, and was firing anti-tank rifles and .50-caliber rounds at our stalled unit. The village was surrounded by a large berme that had been built to protect the plant from monsoon floods.

Our tanks were pinned down by heavy fire and had taken refuge behind the berme. The villagers were running back and forth between the berme and the plant in a panic.

We couldn't conduct a normal attack for fear of injuring villagers. We had to come in very low, behind the berme and tanks. We would then pop up and hold our fire until we were over the civilians, and then begin our attack. They would get a shower of empty machine gun cartridges, but nothing fatal.

The captain began his attack. When he broke off, I fired a rocket to protect his turn. The fire team leader, a young captain, was our new platoon leader. His pilot had only been in country a few days.

I broke my attack and made a steep, quick turn from the target. Enemy fire struck my aircraft. A .50-caliber round came through my window, over my left shoulder, and went out between my crew chief's legs.

He yelled, "We've been hit!" I saw the hole and knew the control rods were under that panel. I turned the aircraft, leveled out, tested the controls, and prepared to crash into a nearby rice paddy.

I worked the controls back and forth. They felt stable. I radioed the lead ship, "I've been hit. I need to dump my ammo." The rookie was flying and turned to continue the attack. Much to my annoyance, he took the same attack path.

I'd just been hit by a .50-caliber coming in from that direction, so I knew they were waiting. I didn't want the same result.

As the rookie broke from his attack, I started my rocket barrage. I swiveled my nose and placed rocket fire from one end of the building to the other, releasing all 12 remaining rockets.

As I broke from my turn, I watched in amazement as the tankers stood up from the protection of the berme.

My rockets had caused a chain reaction. The building had taken some major structural damage and collapsed onto itself. The battle was over; the civilians were safe. We had done our jobs.

After returning to base, I growled at the captain's young pilot for making his second run in the same direction. He apologized and then began to tell me the amazing sight he had seen. As he started his turn from battle, he looked down to see one of my rockets burst below him. He thought, "Good, Doug is right on the job!"

As he continued his turn, he saw a second explosion, then a third, fourth, fifth......twelfth. He looked back at the battle field just as the building collapsed. He said, "I guess you were serious about emptying your ammunition!"

After asking if my controls were OK, the captain headed directly back to base camp. I hovered into the maintenance area and went over the battle damage with the maintenance officer. As my crew chief and I watched, they pulled the panel below his seat.

We could see where the round had entered between his feet, a hole about a half-inch in diameter. As they lifted the aluminum plate, we could see the set of control rods that went from my controls to the transmission. There was not a scratch on either rod, but directly below, there was a hole about 10 inches in diameter where the round had departed the aircraft. The distance between the holes was about 18 inches.

Not a single drop of blood was lost from my crew chief or me, not a scratch on the rods, just one hole in an aluminum plate and one in the aircraft skin.

Prayers in action! I told all this to my church family when I got home. God is faithful, in spite of our flaws! He had placed his mighty protective hand around my aircraft and crew. Thank you, Lord!

The maintenance officer had one of his men cover the outer skin hole with Army-green duct tape, while another replaced the plate. With a smile on his face he said, "Get your aircraft out of my maintenance area. I need the space."

I high-fived my crew chief, then hovered to our parking space. It is interesting to note this battle occurred 24 hours before the start of the Tet Offensive.

I believe our tanks had stumbled on a North Vietnamese unit preparing for the offensive. They were neutralized before they could spring their part of the attack.

CHAPTER ELEVEN
TET (VIETNAM PART 6)

I did a lot of work with the 1st Infantry Division. We flew cover for their outposts when they called for support. When there were major battles, we flew in and out of Lai Khe or Phu Loi, their main base camps.

Loc Ninh was a lonely 1st Infantry outpost. It was divided into two areas, one all South Vietnamese troops, the other, 20 yards away, American. They were built on the Cambodian border, on a hill right where the Ho Chi Minh Trail dumps into South Vietnam. It was the site of many battles with great loss of life. December 10, 1967 was the close of a very vicious battle.

The ARVN half had been overrun, with many casualties. The American side had fought hand to hand and driven off the enemy, with the help of air support. Reinforcements had pushed the enemy back into Cambodia.

My fire team was sent to Loc Ninh a week later. Central Command believed there would soon be another attempt to destroy this vital outpost.

The grass, growing along the edge of the runway, was brown and dry where it sloped into the trees.

My door gunner was standing looking into the trees when he said, "There's something wrong with those trees." I walked over to see where he was looking. The upper branches of several trees were broken, and there a clear substance had flowed down their trunks.

We walked down to the affected trees, where bits of thin aluminum were scattered on the ground. I touched the substance and it was like hardened sap. I broke off a chunk and took it back to my aircraft. It smelled like gasoline. We decided to see if it would burn. It turns out a napalm canister had hit the treetop and split open. Instead of exploding, it had spilled its contents down the trees and solidified.

Liquid napalm burns hot and fast, consuming anything in its path, even air. When it solidifies, it burns like canned Sterno. It turns out it's great for heating cold food.

One of our pilots decided to heat his C-rations (boxed military meals) with a hunk of the newly found cooking aid. He used a lighter to ignite the napalm he'd nestled between several small rocks. Just as the fuel started to burn, another fire team hovered past.

The lead helicopter's rotor wash knocked the napalm stove out of the rocks and set the nearby grass on fire. Our crews started stomping out the fire, trying to protect our helicopters. The pilot who had lit the cooking fire grabbed a fire extinguisher and quickly got the main burn under control.

There was still a small fire burning at the edge of the nearby drainage ditch. I leaned over to see what was burning, just as the pilot extended his extinguisher and sprayed the area. When he pulled his sprayer away, the fire was gone, but suddenly there was a loud hissing sound.

Being an experienced military officer of two years, I knew I did not want to hear a hissing sound, ever.

In Basic Training, the tear gas hissed just before my eyes flowed with burning tears. The hand grenade hissed, just before the sergeant jumped on top of me, protecting me from the potential disaster of my poor toss. My rockets hissed as they rushed from their tubes. Hissing is not good – not when it's that close!

As I pulled away from the sound, I turned to run. Too late! The explosion knocked me to the ground as the sound burst, loudly, in my ears. I picked myself off the ground and began checking to make sure I was still in one piece.

The Lord, again, was merciful! An enemy mortar had hit the inside of the drainage ditch and imbedded into the ground. It had not exploded on impact.

It appears when the Chinese mortar burst from the tube, the fuse had gone out. Our runaway grass fire had reignited the fuse, and BOOM!

Most of the shrapnel went into the ground, but one piece of jagged pot metal struck my left arm and left a bloody eight-inch scratch.

The medic came out to see what had happened. He cleaned the wound and patched me up. No stitches were required, but it left a temporary scar that faded long after my return home.

We stayed at Loc Ninh for several more days. No attack occurred and we left with no further incident.

Next to Christmas, and maybe my birthday, New Year's Day is the most exciting and fun day of the year. New Year's Eve meant going to church for games, singing, being with friends, and waiting for the clock to strike midnight.

New Year's Day was something else altogether. After the Rose Bowl Parade, which we suffered through for mom's sake, came football – lots and lots of college football. It flickered on and on throughout the day and evening.

We saw the Rose, Orange, Sugar, and Sun Bowls. Right in the middle of this feast of magnificent manliness, out came the food. There was ham, turkey, sweet potatoes, and lots of dessert, most left over from Christmas! If there was no company, we got to eat in front of the TV. How could it get any better?

Tet is the Vietnamese New Year. In 1968, it fell on January 30. There was no ham, pie, or football that day.

The 11th was still occupied at the Michelin Rubber Plantation, south of Blackhorse, when we got the call to head for Bien Hoa for redeployment.

On the 31st, 2nd Squadron headed for III Corps POW Camp to back up the unit guarding the compound. It was believed this would be a primary target. It would not be good to have hundreds of prisoners join their comrades in battle.

3rd Squadron moved to An Loc to protect the ARVN headquarters. If the South Vietnamese Army Command fell, there would be no keeping their army together. Part of that unit was sent to U.S. Military Headquarters in Saigon, to aid in their defense.

1st Squadron moved north towards the DMZ (demilitarized zone).

My part of Air Cav was sent to protect the 1st Infantry Division Headquarters in Phu Loi. My friend Rob was stationed there.

He told me to relax – there hadn't been any attacks on this base in months. I was ready for a good night's sleep. Blackhorse had taken mortar attacks, every hour on the hour, a few rounds at a time, the last few nights. We hadn't gotten much sleep.

Our helicopters were parked about 50 yards from our concrete barracks. I spent most of my nights in a field tent or inside my aircraft. Sleeping in a real bed was quite a treat.

Rob and I had been at the officers' club for a nice hot meal and a good visit. After we finished, he took me where I was to stay while at 1st Infantry Division Headquarters. It was a nice brick building with comfortable beds and clean sheets. It even had night stands. The best part was no red dirt!

I was sound asleep when the first mortar hit. I sat up in bed, not sure where I was! Rob had shown me the bunker, but for the life of me I couldn't remember where it was. My junior pilot was in the bed across the room, mumbling incoherently.

I yelled, "We better get to the bunker!" I opened the bedroom door and turned left to get outside. We were in the first room inside the officers' quarters. I grabbed the handle and pulled the brown metal door wide open. I was about to take a step outside when there was a sudden flash and deafening explosion.

My first reaction was to close the door. The problem was, 20 men were charging down the hallway. The door slammed shut just as the first of the chargers reached us.

I remember being slammed against the door and then being pushed forward through the now reopened passageway. My feet never seemed to touch the ground as the desperate mob pushed forward like a tidal wave.

The ride stopped as my body, still in an upright position, was slammed into the bunker's back wall. I crumpled to the bottom of the bunker and began praying. It was very comforting to know that the God of this universe was right there holding my little mortal hand.

There is a saying among soldiers, "There are no atheists in foxholes." The sounds I heard that night coming from the 20 plus men stuffed in that damp bunker were not, "There is no God!"

The scariest part of the whole ordeal was lying in the bottom of the bunker, listening to the mortars landing all around, praying none would enter the bunker.

I had never experienced fear as I did in those 20 minutes. I had times when I was growing up that I had been frightened by threats from "tough guys." I see those as learning experiences that toughened me up. I had felt shame for not standing up to them, and didn't like it, so I had to either toughen up, or feel like a wimp the rest of my life. I chose not to feel that way anymore. No! I didn't go looking for trouble, but I also didn't run scared anymore.

The fear I experienced that night had no shame attached. This was war, and fear was programmed into every single moment. The experience brought me closer to the Lord, and his protective power, and I love him the more for it.

When the attack ended, someone looked at me and said, "You're bleeding!" My co-pilot was also bleeding from a deep gash on his forehead. We were taken to the base clinic where I was treated for minor scratches and shrapnel wounds, from head to toe. Fortunately, my co-pilot's forehead needed no stitches.

When I first opened the door, the mortar hit not more than 20 feet in front of me. My co-pilot had been behind me and the door, so he had not been hit by the flying dirt and metal.

His wound had occurred as we had been pushed into the bunker. His head hit the metal revetment used to hold the sandbags above the bunker.

Looking back on this experience, I had no doubt the prayers of my family and friends kept not only me, but my whole unit safe in God's care.

My co-pilot that night was the same one who had been flying the lead aircraft when my ship took the .50-caliber round. He became a very good pilot. Maybe my scolding had done some good.

That night the mortars fell between my bedroom and my aircraft. There were no direct hits. Thank you, Lord!

When we returned, all patched up from the clinic, we headed for our aircraft to make sure our crew and helicopter were in one piece. The crew had taken cover behind the revetment that protected our helicopter, and were shaken but not injured.

It was a little rough putting on my flight suit and helmet, but we were being called to assistance in repelling ongoing attacks. Good old Rob had spotted some mortar positions and needed my handy-dandy little fire team to rain down some havoc.

Rob had taken his slick and was trying to locate the mortar position that had interrupted my beautiful, deep, peaceful sleep. There would be nothing better, as far as I was concerned, than to return the favor that night. I took my team to Rob's position, but the Air Force had arrived before us.

The FAC told us to hold to the east. We were flying just below the clouds at 500 feet. I looked back at my crew and saw my door gunner turn white as a sheet, which was pretty bad since he was a young black male. He was pointing out his door and saying, "Jet! Jet! Jet!" I looked where he was pointing just in time to see the jet drop his bombs and pull out of his dive.

He didn't see us until the last second; I broke down left as he rolled up and over my tail and into the clouds.

My door gunner told me later he could read "Steve Canyon" on his helmet. He was that close.

One of the more unsavory things that happened because of Tet was that the Vietcong received rockets from the Chinese. These rockets were not huge, but with practice they became deadly accurate.

Rob had been ordered to find the local launching position that had been firing on 1st Infantry Headquarters, and stop the attacks. He told me he had flown round and round Phu Loi and spotted a potential location. He called me to bring my fire team and try to put the lights out on these attacks.

The next attack occurred during daylight. Rob got his helicopter airborne and alerted me of the attack. I was already in the air not far from Phu Loi, so dispatching this site had not been that difficult. Good job, Rob!

I had been flying missions protecting Blackhorse Base Camp and been on-call for nearby units. Rocket attacks at Phu Loi had stopped so Rob had not called for nearly a week.

I was preparing for evening patrol when I received an alert that Bien Hoa Air Base was under rocket attack. I was flying wing for my new platoon leader.

We headed off into the deepening night as quickly as we could, but the Air Force beat us there. The site had gone silent when they heard the jets arrive.

The FAC told us to circle off to the south until the jets were finished. We were a mile off when the FAC told us to move in; the jets were finished.

I had fallen back from the leader. In case he took fire from the ground, I would be in a better position to return it.

As we proceeded forward, the enemy made a fatal mistake. The captain didn't realize, but his aircraft had flown over the rocket launcher. As he passed by, the enemy launched a rocket right over his aircraft.

The bright flash of the rocket's exhaust gave me a clear look at my target. Without even thinking, I lowered my nose and launched six rockets of my own.

I had one shot at my target. It was a very dark, moonless night, and by the time we returned for another pass, darkness had again returned to the enemy's position.

The next morning a search team went out and recovered a load of rockets, the launcher, and 28 enemy bodies.

Although Tet officially lasted until late February, the majority of the fighting was over in the first two weeks. We had been involved in an almost unending series of missions during those two weeks.

When the main battles had ended, we were sent home to our tents at Blackhorse, and back to the steady on-call routine.

50 years later, I was talking to a 1st Infantry soldier who had been on the ground during Tet. His unit had been pinned down during the early battle, and was calling for gunship support, but was informed there was none available. "Hunker down and hold on," they were told. "We'll get to you as soon as possible!"

I said, "I'm sorry. We were very, very busy those first few days." He said he understood and that they had fought their way out of the mess, like many others that night.

As a senior flight officer, I was added to the night command rotation. The night command was in charge of the whole post for the entire night – just me and a duty sergeant. For one night, I was going to command the 11th Armored Cavalry and its 2,000 men. This isn't as important as it sounds – any decisions I made would be about night guard duty, but it still sounds good on a resume.

I reported to headquarters at dusk. The sergeant met me as I arrived and walked me through my responsibilities. I actually had a bed in one of the rooms if I wanted to take a nap. It was going to be a long night!

If there was an emergency call, it would come to this office. We would take the information: location, contact frequency, and casualties. One of us would push the "alert team" button that would send the "30-second" team into action. When they were airborne, we would give them the information garnered from the caller.

Every few hours, the sergeant and I got into a jeep and drove around camp. We stopped at each guard post to inspect and make sure everyone was awake.

Sometime around 1:00 a.m., we were called to a guard post that had seen movement. We had no patrols out, so I gave them permission to fire. We watched for several minutes, shined lights, and fired several more times. Nothing!

We had alerted the other guard posts in case this was a ruse, and the real attack would be elsewhere. Nothing more happened, so we returned to headquarters. All was quiet the rest of the night. I never did get a nap or push the "alert team" button. Just as well, peace and quiet was just fine!

The next morning, a patrol found a dead kangaroo where we'd fired the night before! The nearby Australian camp had reported their pet "Roo" had escaped a few days earlier. We found it. Sorry!

As senior aircraft commander, I was assigned the duty of armament officer. With that duty, headquarters classified me with "Crypto" clearance. Crypto is top secret/sensitive compartmented information. Very hush-hush!

My job was to fly aircraft to Vung Tau, the Army's maintenance depot on the coast, and get new secret radios and weapons fitted to our gunships. I was to stay until the work was done, then test them before returning home. Upon return, I taught the other pilots how to use our new equipment.

On my first trip, I took 522 to get fitted for new weapons – Miniguns.

Our new mini guns

It required replacing the pylons that held the M60s, and re-fitting the electrical connections. After a few hours work, the maintenance officer had me take 522 out to test the refit.

I flew a few miles off the coast to test my new machine guns. As I was picking a good spot, I noticed the sea was a strange brownish color and not moving the way ocean water normally does.

I turned the aircraft around and dropped down for a better look. Closer examination showed snakes—big ugly brown snakes—by the millions. Well, I hadn't tested my guns, so naturally I shot right into that squirming brown mass.

I found out later it was breeding time. Every known variety of poisonous sea snake lives off the coast of Vietnam and breeds there once a year. I'm glad I never took any of my downtime swimming in those waters.

The last few weeks in Vietnam were not nearly as eventful as the other 11½ months. Tet had taken most of the fight out of the enemy. We were back to local patrols, road clearing, and protecting local clinic work.

On March 16, 1968, I flew my last mission in the Republic of Vietnam. On March 26th, I boarded a UH-1 slick, and was flown to Bien Hoa Air Force Base.

On March 28, 1968, I boarded a commercial jet to San Francisco. I was nervous, excited, and ready to see my family. We flew by way of Japan, then "over the top" – the North Pole to Anchorage. In Alaska the temperature was 34 degrees! It was 90 degrees in Saigon.

During the week before my departure, I began the "de-Vietnaming" process. The military likes to control everything.

I had shots and physicals to go to Vietnam; now I had to have my shots checked and a departure physical.

They also gave me a supply of malaria pills, enough to last eight weeks after I arrived home. I had to take 60 big orange pills, two middle-sized pills, and two little bitty ones.

I received new orders a few days before departing Vietnam: Fort Wolters, Texas, here I come!

As I was packing my duffle bag, I stepped out of the tent to retrieve a rocket box I used to store my extra gear. As I reached for the box, which was between the dusty green tent and brown sandbags, a flash of green caught my eye. I jerked back just in time to see a bamboo viper coiled to strike.

Bamboo vipers are called "three-step vipers" because that's how long you have until the toxin paralyzes your muscles, including your heart and lungs.

I backed away from the lurking danger and called my roommates to see what was living outside the front door. The viper was still next to the sandbag. One of my roommates had a bow and arrow tucked away in his personals, so he brought it out. After three shots, he had dispatched the angry snake before it could do any harm.

It was large for a viper, probably from eating all the local rats. It was four feet long and so thick around its middle that my hand could barely reach around it. The bright fluorescent-green color, shining in the afternoon sun, was not diminished in death.

With bags packed, I waited on the tarmac for my ride to Bien Hoa. As I was waiting to board the outbound helicopter, a brand-new Cobra hovered over and landed on the next pad. These two-man aircraft were just beginning to arrive in Vietnam and would soon replace 522. New pilots arriving in country would be prepared to use these new machines to take the battle to our enemy.

I walked over and talked to the pilots. They let me sit in the gunner's seat that hung out over the nose of this powerful machine. This was my one and only contact with the Army's newest flying gun platform. The Cobra, and later the Apache, slowly replaced the UH-1C as the Army's aerial gun platform.

I was finally headed home. Thank you, Lord, for your all-powerful protective hand of mercy!

Chapter Twelve
R&R and Fauna

I would be remiss if I didn't give kudos to the U.S. military for the care and concern they showed for the mental health of their troops. Don't get me wrong, they took us away from home and family, and put us in harm's way, but they physically and mentally prepared us as best they could.

During my Vietnam duty, I had several opportunities to get away from the stress of war, at least for a while.

We each had a one-weekend pass to one of the larger cities nearby. The military had semi-protected areas that had local food, shopping, and scenery.

I spent my weekend in Saigon. There was little to no cost and the food was great, especially if you liked rice dishes. The U.S. military ran and guarded the Grand Hotel in the downtown area, inside the secure zone.

The Vietcong were masters of disguise – you never knew who was a friendly or an enemy. Civilians and Vietcong all looked and dressed the same. You might see a young woman dressed in an "ao dai" (traditional dress), or an old man with a conical hat and worn-work clothing. If you had to choose the enemy, nothing set them apart from anyone else nearby. The woman could be a spy checking military strength, or the man could be carrying explosives. It was important to be alert at all times.

I bought a lot of neat carved ivory pieces from local shops. The ivory was imported from Africa; it was legal in the 1960s. There were very few elephants in Vietnam.

The military also ran a water-skiing area just outside the city. We could watch the fun during warm weather and every time I flew a mission that brought us close to the Dong Nai River. They had several ski boats and lots of water skis to help take the skier's mind off the war.

I heard about other places: in the north, the Imperial City of Hue, and to the south, Vung Tau on the coast offered a three-day safe and free refuge to tired troops. A squad of our tank troops took a three-day "R&R" (rest and relaxation) in Vung Tau, but they forgot to buy sunscreen. One of them said, "Let's use transmission fluid. There's lots of that." The whole group suffered from acid burns for weeks, much to their commanding officer's dismay.

The military also offered seven days of R&R abroad for those who had the money for room and board. Each month a list of available places and spaces would be sent to the units. Everyone who had not taken an R&R had the opportunity, by seniority, to take any of the offered trips. My door gunner enjoyed a well-earned trip to Hong Kong.

When my turn arrived, sometime in September of 1967, I chose to go to Bangkok, Thailand. It took less than two hours to fly the 447 miles between Saigon and Bangkok.

I was not allowed to wear my military uniform, since even though I was out of the war zone, there was still danger of reprisal or kidnapping by local communist sympathizers. Before I left, my unit gave me information on the best sites to see, forms of travel, and dangers to avoid.

Arriving in the afternoon, I caught a cab that took me to the hotel where I had reserved a room. I was glad to hear the hotel's staff speaking in fluent English. Before arriving in Vietnam, I'd never been out of the United States, so I had no other external reference.

After settling my gear, I set about exploring my surroundings. There was a nice swimming pool, a restaurant, and plenty of advice from the hotel staff.

I was on a steep learning curve of what not to do. My first mistake was taking anything valuable to the swimming pool. I thought it would be safe leaving my watch in an unsecured locker, rolled in my pants. Nope! I knew I was in trouble when I saw a staff member go into the locker room as I came out.

When I finished my swim, my watch was gone! Glad I hadn't brought any money! Oh well. Watches are cheap in the PX back at Blackhorse. I had better things to do than swim, anyway.

Dinner time! Off to the hotel restaurant. The menu had lots of local flare, but "Southern Fried Chicken and Banana" definitely caught my eye. I just couldn't pass up that unseemly combination.

Wow! I was hooked! I was enjoying the perfectly fried chicken when my fork caught a piece of banana. My mouth couldn't take in this unfamiliar taste…oh, yeah, banana – plantain to be exact. It was delicious!

Thailand is a Buddhist nation. Most of South East Asia is controlled by Buddhism. Everywhere you look you will see the orange-robed men and boys who move about their work under the supervision of their overseers. They were generally in groups of three.

Thailand is a kingdom that has a monarch, but it also has one of Asia's most magnificent collections of Buddhist temples.

I didn't want to be seen as a tourist, so it occurred to me, "Why not take the bus?" In America I drove my car, or took the bus, so why not get a bus schedule and enjoy the ride?

I found the local bus stop with its city map, and waited for the appropriately-numbered transport to arrive. The door opened and I dropped a seven-cent token into the till. I reached the top of the steps and turned to find myself the center of attention. Every seat was taken and standing room was at a premium.

Here I was, a six-foot American, standing in a line of five-foot Asian males, all dressed in black slacks and white dress shirts. I can only guess what was going through their minds: "What is this rich American doing riding a bus?"

The tension eased quickly and the chatter rose as the bus resumed its route. I disembarked at the palace exit and entered the Royal Grounds. Camera in hand, I returned to being a tourist.

There were artists scattered around the grounds working at their individual skills. I noticed there were many on their hands and knees against one of the temple walls.

After photographing the pink and gold-colored palace, curiosity took me to the kneeling artists. Each artist had a wooden box full of multicolored pieces of chalk. Next to the box was a stack of rice paper. I watched in awe as the nearest artist covered his finger in chalk and gently rubbed against the rice paper that was taped to the wall.

I glanced at the next artist and noticed the temple wall was covered in carvings. Each pictured a different scene of war elephants, fighting, parading, or charging into battle. Their warriors, spears in hand, were standing in a gilded box fastened to the elephant's back.

The pictures were reminders of fierce battles fought in Thailand's glorious past.

As the artist in front of me finished his rubbing, I asked if it was for sale. He requested 75 cents and I gladly produced the funds that would feed his family for a day. I gently rolled the delicate picture in another piece of paper and headed off to my next adventure.

I should have purchased more and mailed them home. So much for hindsight! I was ready to search out the temples that enclosed the Jade Buddha, Reclining Buddha, and the Solid Gold Buddha.

The Jade Buddha, also known as the Emerald Buddha, was carved from a piece of jade or jasper, and stands 26 inches tall. It's clothed in gold leaf, and is Thailand's most sacred statue. I had to view it from outside the open door. Light from windows above the statue made it shine in the morning sun.

The Reclining Buddha is 150 feet long and is also plated in gold. It is housed in a huge building that contains over 1,000 other Buddha images. I was struck by the number of candles that had been lit by worshipers across from the image's resting place. So many lost souls grasping for hope in the wrong place.

History, legend, and a sign outside the Solid Gold Buddha's temple tells us that during an invasion, the monks covered the four-ton gold statue with a concrete and plaster camouflage. It was taken to an out-of-the-way temple and painted. It went undiscovered for 200 years, until the temple was falling apart.

They had to move the Buddha to a new temple in Bangkok. It was put in a discrete spot because it was so ugly. It couldn't be destroyed because it was a Buddha!

At some point, a piece of concrete plaster broke loose and the gold became visible. The bright shiny statue is now visible, also from the doorway, for all to see.

No visit to Thailand is complete without a visit to the elephant park to ride one of those enormous creatures.

After paying my 25 cents, I climbed a set of steps that brought me level to the box attached to the elephant's back. I climbed aboard and held on tight as the handler led his charge around the designated path and back to our loading area.

Temple rubbing from Thailand

What's it like to ride an elephant? Picture yourself riding atop a fat, stinky, tugboat, swaying side to side as it lumbers perpendicular to an ocean wave. I'm glad I hadn't eaten before climbing aboard.

After my ride, I was walking through the park and noticed a heavily-wired area with a small hill in the center. Atop the hill was a king cobra sunning itself in the warm afternoon sun.

As I watched, it lifted its enormous head and spread its cowl in an open display of irritation. King cobras can reach 18 feet in length and weigh 20 to 28 pounds. It was an awesome sight, and I felt honored to be a witness to this wonderful display of God's creation.

One last thing I wanted to do was purchase some black opals. I had established a friendship with one of the hotel clerks and asked him where I could find a good deal on opals. He had a cousin that drove a taxi; he had taken me to several scenic locations at a price lower than other taxis. He must have received a percentage from the places I made my purchases. I spent a lot!

He said, "I have a cousin that owns a jewelry shop. If you like, my other cousin can take you there in his taxi and introduce you."

I did get a great deal on black opals. I purchased 20 good-sized ones and had them put into tie tacks and necklaces for our wedding party. I still have several loose stones in my jewelry box.

It was a relaxing, enjoyable trip, but it was time to go back to work.

In late January, after Tet had run its course, they sent out a new R&R list. There was still one trip available after everyone had a chance. I was asked if I was interested.

On February 8, 1968, I boarded a plane for Sydney, Australia. One of the blessings of not being a drinker, I still had money.

It was an eight-hour flight to Darwin, then four more to Sydney. Darwin is on the equator; it was very hot, dry, and covered in red dirt.

After fire opals were discovered, miners began digging underground tunnels to mine the newfound treasure. The tunnels were more than just mines; they proved to be a great place to escape the often unbearable heat. The locals started building their homes and even businesses below ground in the much cooler mines.

Sydney is a beautiful city. I told my future bride it looks like a "clean San Francisco." My hotel room overlooked the harbor and I could see the unfinished opera building.

As the night set in, lights outlined the dark waters of the natural harbor. The moonlight reflected off the still waters. I wish my future life's partner had been there to see it; it was a master painting from the Master himself.

My hotel was in the city center, so I was out the front door and experiencing the highlights of this beautiful city.

Trusty camera in my pocket, I made every effort to avoid looking like a tourist. It didn't work. As I passed a wool shop, the owner stepped out and said, "Howdy, Yank! Come see my shop." He grabbed my arm and quick as a wink I was trying on beautiful, handmade Australian wool sweaters.

I felt fortunate to have gotten out with just one 17-dollar beautiful, soft, brown wool sweater, which I wore for many years.

When I returned to the hotel, I was met by the hotel manager. He asked me if I would be willing to move from my room. A cruise ship had arrived a few days early and they desperately needed my room. I had no problem, so he sent a bellboy who helped me pack and then took me to another room.

We stepped off the elevator into the penthouse. I was now rooming with three other Americans. We each had our own private room. A full kitchen, a fully-stocked fridge, and the living room took up the rest of the hotel's top floor. The view took in all of Sydney, including the harbor. The night view was beyond awesome. Not bad for 25 dollars a night.

In the center of Sydney was a park to beat all parks. The grass was meticulously manicured, dark green, and beautiful. Lawn bowlers, in groups of eight, were scattered all around the manicured field. There were lakes, trees, carriage rides, and young lovers in abundance. It looked like San Francisco's Golden Gate Park or Central Park in New York.

It was dinner time, so I headed back to the hotel. I've found in foreign countries the major hotels have great cooks. I was not disappointed; they had sweet and sour pork with rice. Sounded right up my alley, so I had to give it a try. They brought out a large platter of pork and seconds later a platter of steamed rice.

I was happily munching away when I was brought to a stop by a very spicy piece of pork. My mouth, throat, and stomach warmed and my tongue started calling for more. I slowly ate the rest of the meal and decided I had to come back for lunch tomorrow. Three times that week I gorged on that incredible meal. The spicy piece of pork was in every meal, but never in the same spot.

I woke up one morning and my left arm was swollen. I called the military liaison and he got me an appointment with an Australian military doctor. I put on my uniform, and a taxi took me to the Sydney military fort. The attending doctor knew immediately what was wrong: I had been bitten by a spider.

He gave me a cream to put on my arm and told me to go back to my room, shower, put on the salve, and take a nap. When I woke, the swelling was gone!

He told me when I rubbed the salve on, it would make my whole body warm and I'd get a taste like oysters in my mouth. I've heard this stuff isn't legal in the States. I wish it was; it works great on almost every ache and pain.

The Sydney museum and zoo were touted as a must-see. It was much like the de Young Museum in Golden Gate Park. It doesn't have the giant Kodiak bear that makes your hair stand on end as you go through the front door, but it has lots of cool things to see.

The real thrill was in the live animal and arboreal display. They had a real live platypus! I didn't realize how large they are, or that the males have a venomous spur on their back leg. They also lay eggs. Wow! What an awesome God we have!

The hotel offered a one-day horseback trip into the outback. We rode along a canyon trail among the tall eucalyptus trees. There were 20 of us, in single file, as we pushed deeper into the Australian wild. Off to my right, the canyon fell steeply away. After three hours, we made it back to the stables and I spent the rest of the day soaking my saddle sores.

I didn't see any wild koalas or kangaroos, but there had been lots of those at the zoo. On February 15, 1968, I boarded the plane that took me back to Darwin and then Saigon.

I had six more weeks until I would be going home.

I've mentioned snakes, spiders, birds, and water buffalo, but there are many other creatures in Vietnam.

I was on patrol one morning and decided to give the stream just west of Blackhorse a good once over. It was an ideal camping spot, with plenty of water. I noticed what I thought was a large tree laying across one of the many ponds along the small stream.

I turned my team to take another look; there were no trees that large anywhere near this area. I slowed my airspeed and came in at treetop level.

What I first thought was a very large tree was in fact an enormous crocodile. Its head was resting on one bank and a portion of the tail on the opposite. My aircraft was around 40 feet long and wouldn't have quite fit in the pond. I was not about to stop and measure the monster.

He was laying on a game trail and must have had plenty to eat. My guess was he had ventured up the creek as a youngster and found the pickings to his liking. He was now much too large to leave his tree-lined prison.

We talked about what to do about him. We normally didn't send patrols to this area and he was definitely a threat to any enemy, so we left him to his morning nap.

I reported his presence on my after-action report. What Command decided I never found out.

I flew many missions in the Central Highlands, where the Montagnard (Degar) live. They are an indigenous people that live a simple village life. They hunt with handmade crossbows and poison arrows. Monkeys, antelope, and birds are their main food source.

We were on a recon mission in the Highlands, ahead of one of our troops, when we spotted a troop of monkeys. They were swinging through the jungle top trying to escape our giant, noisy birds.

Their long, shiny, black hair swept back as they desperately followed their leader. Along their sides were streaks of red, blue, and yellow that glistened in the midday sun. It was a truly beautiful sight! We followed until they dropped into the jungle and disappeared.

When I said the Montagnard hunted antelope, I didn't mean American-sized antelope, which can weigh over 90 pounds. Vietnamese deer are called "dik-diks." They weigh in around 6 to 13 pounds.

We had one that lived in a clump of bamboo near my tent. It went running by one afternoon. It didn't run like any other four-legged animal – it skipped. It looked like it was flying. One minute it was there, the next it was gone.

Even the ugliest birds had a unique beauty. I was flying one afternoon, heading for home, when we came up behind a large, slow-moving bird. The closer we got, the uglier it looked.

It had dark brown feathers, long spindly legs hanging below its skinny body, and a wrinkly neck. There was a long turkey gobbler hunk of skin that hung from its chin. It was ugly! The striking thing was the color of its neck and head – they were a beautiful yellow.

For awhile we did have pets at Blackhorse. There was a monkey, until it escaped. It was already there when I arrived so I have no idea where it came from. We also had a "free-range" chicken.

Whoever bought it thought it was a hen, and was hoping for fresh eggs. Turns out roosters don't lay eggs, but they do "crow" early in the morning. If it hadn't been for the fact the chicken liked to hunt and eat big red spiders, he would have lost his head long ago. When the rainy season ended, the spiders went back to the ground and the rooster became a nuisance.

One morning, the rooster's crowing woke one of our senior officers; he'd been on a long night mission the night before and was not happy. The next day, I flew a morning mission with that same officer. He captured the offender and handed him to our crew chief, who had also complained of the rooster's noise.

Several miles from Blackhorse, above a dense portion of the jungle, the crew chief set the rooster free. We watched as the rooster spread his short stubby wings and gently glided to a safe landing in a small clearing. The last we saw, he was running full speed into the dark green jungle.

There was a huge sigh of relief the next morning when dawn arrived to peace and quiet.

Another time, we landed in a large field one of our tank units had chosen for a night bivouac. I was hovering to our night landing area, when my crew chief yelled, "Look out!" I saw a banana bush on my right just as the rotor took out its top.

I shut the engine down and slowed the rotor until we could see what damage had been done. The bush had cleaned a wide swatch across both blades with no damage. I took a knife and cut into the rest of the bush and found it was soft and fibrous. My crew chief pulled the dislodged top to the aircraft, and cut off the attached bunch of bananas.

Bananas attract big, nasty, hairy, biting spiders that hide among the fruit. We hung the bananas outside our tent until they ripened and the spiders left. It was worth the wait.

CHAPTER THIRTEEN
HOME

Walking into the plane, I could feel the excitement welling inside. I found a window seat and settled in for the long, long flight over the North Pole to Alaska, where we would refuel.

I was dressed comfortably in my short-sleeve military khakis; it was a very hot day!

The gray cement tarmac reflected the hot Saigon sun. I watched as the Air Force crewmen finished their preflight, and locked the luggage doors.

Before we were cleared to leave, an information officer came aboard to give us a reentry talk. When we first arrived in Vietnam, the information officer gave us a packet that told us about Vietnam, its customs, and people. Reentry talks are just what it says. No information packet was needed; we were about to reenter American society after a year in a war zone.

The military was concerned about the negativity soldiers had been receiving upon their return home. They also wanted to make sure we were not trying to sneak contraband into the country.

The information officer said, "Be prepared to be yelled at, called baby killers, and even spat on. The world you left has changed in the time you have been in Vietnam."

None of us were prepared for what we were hearing. One of my fellow passengers asked, "Should we be wearing our uniforms? What should we do if someone attacks us? I don't know if I can control myself! I've been fighting for my life here. I may start throwing blows."

After fighting for our country and its freedoms, this was a real letdown. The mumbling grew louder!

119

I was a little concerned because my family and friends were going to meet me at the San Francisco Airport. How would they handle me being yelled at or mocked?

We arrived in Anchorage early the next morning. We were told to wait in the airport lounge while our plane was refueled. The airport ground crew rolled out a movable stair; there was no covered walkway due to the heavy snow. The cold air met me, and my short-sleeved khaki shirt, like a ton of frozen bricks. We ran like Olympic racers to the lounge. It was only 40 yards but seemed like miles.

The five-hour flight to San Francisco was full of concern and I prayed a lot, but the Lord is in control. A good-sized crowd met me alright, but they were all family and friends. I was home!

I was now on a well-earned, 10-weeks paid vacation!

For the first week, my time was spent visiting friends, helping finish plans, and rehearsing for April 13, 1968. That was the day I left bachelorhood and Peggy Ellen King became Peggy Ellen Eggerth! She was so beautiful walking down the aisle, supported lovingly on her dad's arm.

After honeymooning in the beautiful confines of snowy Yosemite National Park, we came home for a final visit with friends and family.

I had seven weeks vacation before we were to report to Fort Wolters, Texas, where I would become an instructor pilot. I would be going back where flight school began.

We were anxious to head to Texas and begin a home of our own. That home ended up being a nice duplex in a wooded corner of the peaceful hamlet of Mineral Wells. Peaceful, that is, until the beehive called Fort Wolters sprang to life just around dawn.

On a warm, sunny April day, as our ancestors had done before us, we loaded our worldly goods into a four-wheeled covered vehicle, kissed our families goodbye, and headed off to Texas. Our 1966 Ford Mustang shouldered the load, pulled its weight, and brought us safely down the long road to our new home.

Instructor training introduced me to a new helicopter. The Hughes 500 was a small, orange, two-man machine that looked like a fat dragonfly. It had a short tail with small thin rotor blades.

We didn't fly in the rain; the tail rotors blades would get heavy pits when struck by large rain drops or hail. The pits caused the thin blades to vibrate and need replacing.

It was produced for the military by The Howard Hughes Corporation. One of Peggy's brothers worked there as an engineer.

Hughes 500, my new training helicopter

A day's training, learning the feel and controls of a new helicopter, heliport flight patterns, and local land contour, then a flight test, and I was a military instructor pilot. The scariest part was doing a 360-degree backup autorotation to a five-foot pad in an aircraft I'd only flown for two hours. This new chopper was fun to fly. It was small and responded quickly to the barest touch of its controls. My gunship had been like flying a tank. This was a Porsche!

I was assigned to an Advanced Basic Flight Training group.
I was one of two shiny new rookie instructor pilots. The other guy was first through the door, so he was assigned as the flight safety officer. My assignment was not so glamorous. I don't even remember what the duty entailed.

The thing about safety officer, if there's an accident in the unit, the job goes to the next lowest officer. That would be me!

Two weeks later, after a student had a minor accident, I became the new safety officer! I held that job until the day I left the military, 20 months later!

Each week I gave the students a safety lecture. If a student had an emergency, I went to evaluate the situation and determine how to handle it.

My first instruction to the students was, "If you think something's wrong, get on the ground. I'll come and check it out." It kept me busy, but the unit accident free.

I was assigned three students at a time. Most were young Army recruits, like I had been.

We would fly in three rotating shifts, mornings from 6:00 a.m. to 10:00 a.m.; afternoons, 1:00 p.m. to 5:00 p.m., and nights, 6:00 p.m. to 10:00 p.m. Each shift would be for three weeks as we taught the assigned skills.

When the students flew mornings, they had school in the afternoons, and when they flew afternoons, they had school in the morning. Night flying usually had school in the afternoon as well.

As an instructor, I was off during the non-flying hours, unless I was in the middle of an investigation or loaded with paperwork.

The Army also trained Marine officers and Iranians! One of those Iranians was the Shah's personal pilot. He had been trained to fly everything but helicopters, and was fluent in six languages. It was sad to hear he may have been murdered when the Shah was overthrown.

When a student got lost, the safety officer and his instructor had to find him. Many times, I was called by the flight commander, as I was out with one of my own students, to help find a student lost in the grand expanse of East Texas. When away from the local landmarks, it was easy to lose oneself in the rolling hills, miles of mesquite, juniper, and prickly pear cactus.

Once, two young Marine officers got lost flying cross country south of Fort Wolters. They landed near a gas station and called the base. They asked if they could buy some regular gas and fly home. The regular gas would have exploded the engine when it mixed with aviation fuel! My student and I had to fly out several gallons of fuel to get them safely home.

Another lost student landed in a farm yard just before dark. When we located him, after dark, we landed near his aircraft and walked to the farmhouse to check in with the owners. One of us knocked as the other looked through the farmhouse window. Two elderly ladies were watching the red and white lights rotating and flashing in their pasture. They hadn't seen the second aircraft, or its pilots walking to their front door. At the sound of the knock, both ladies nearly jumped out of their skins. They must have thought it was an invasion from outer space.

Regaining their composure, both ladies approached and slowly opened the door. I explained, "One of our students got lost and picked your pasture as a safe place to land! I apologize for disturbing your evening. We'll remove the aircraft as soon as possible." In typical Texas grace, the two elderly women accepted our apology and said, "It's quite alright! Is your student OK? Would you like to come in for some cookies and tea?" I thanked them for the offer but responded, "We have to get our student home, but thank you very much for your offer."

We had arrived in late April. By the end of July, I had trained my first class and my new wife had found a job working as a waitress: $1.50 an hour, plus tips.

The menu included T-bone steak, ranch beans, and a veggie for $1.50. The local ranchers would bring their wives to town for a nice Saturday meal of Swiss steak and mashed potatoes for $1.75. Texas ranchers were big spenders in those days.

My wife loved to walk to work and enjoyed the quiet life we lived in Mineral Wells.

But not everything went the way she liked! Crickets, lots and lots of crickets, were her worst nemesis. Normally they stayed out of sight, but when the weather changed, they seemed to be everywhere. They were in our house, floating in the swimming pool, and always singing their endless song.

The continual squeaking sound was bad enough, but it was their jumping that drove her to distraction. With her every step, they would be crushed underfoot, or jump up under her cotton dress, landing on her legs and driving her crazy. Pants were not an option for young ladies in the 1960s.

When I saw crickets, I saw blue gill, crappie, and bass: fish, lots and lots of fish, since crickets are their favorite meal.

Fortunately, the infestation only lasted a few weeks and she was back in her happy place, walking the quiet, friendly, small town streets of Mineral Wells.

August through November, I fought the weather with my students while my little bride got a job in a doctor's office. We also bought a single-wide mobile home. The home came with a king-size bed, was completely furnished, and was placed right next to the swimming pool. No one used the pool but us and the owner's young son and daughter. It was cute to have them come to the door and ask if we would come out and play. We rarely disappointed our two favorite neighbors.

Accident investigation was another duty safety officers pulled. I served off and on with the Fort's investigation team for the rest of my time at Wolters.

There were six safety officers for Advanced Basic and we rotated each time there was an accident or incident. Serving on the team didn't exempt me from flying with my students. It was added work but it sure made the days go quickly.

Accidents and incidents are common in regular military units, and in student units they more than double. The Lord was merciful to our unit – no accidents, no paperwork!

The more serious the accident, the more the paperwork. When there was a fatality, the investigation could take months, many hours of interviews, tests, and report writing. We would travel to the accident scene, often in the middle of nowhere, make observations, and photograph the whole area.

Each aircraft had extensive records of maintenance, pilot reports, and observations. Sitting for hours reading log books was never my idea of fun, but trying to make sense of a metallurgy report, done when damaged metal is involved, is real headache material.

All the skills I learned examining, observing, and questioning came in handy during the 20 plus years I spent working with juvenile delinquents after the military.

Wearing earplugs every time I climbed into my turbine-powered death machine actually increased my hearing, much to the frustration of those same young troublemakers.

During one flight with a student, we received a mayday call on our emergency frequency; it came from an Air Force jet a mile south of our location! He had a flameout engine failure, and was trying to land in the shallow, sandy, tree-lined Brazos River.

We quickly located his position and answered his mayday call. I had my student line up with his flight path and we followed his slow, gliding descent.

We listened to the chatter between the pilot and his flight controller. He radioed, "I'm going to try to set her down in the Brazos. It seems shallow and sandy. I'm headed into the wind! There's an Army helicopter following me down. I'm going to attempt one more restart!"

We were prepared to render aid and help in his recovery. We watched, with a sigh of relief, as he was able to restart the engine just seconds before crashing. It was a great, unexpected training moment.

Several hundred miles from Mineral Wells is an Air Force B-52 training base. If you look at a military or Department of Defense aviation map, you will see thin black lines that are marked "oil burner" routes. These lines are low-level navigation training routes. The Air Force keeps these routes away from high population areas and airfields. The closest "oil burner" route was over 100 miles west of Mineral Wells.

One afternoon, I was out with one of my students doing field landings. These practice landings were done on small open spaces just large enough for one aircraft, away from any permanent airfields,

As a student and I were lifting off one of these small fields, we heard an excited call from our stage field, where I had left my other students practicing solo flying.

According to the stage field tower, an Air Force B-52 bomber had flown low level over our practice field.

One of our instructors said the helicopters were "dancing like butterflies in a windstorm" in the B-52's wake. The B-52 was only 120 miles off course. Go, Air Force!

Practice landing fields were usually surrounded by scrub trees, or next to obstacles such as hills, streams, or cliffs. They were located on both public and private lands and marked with colored tires.

White tires marked landing areas for all students, yellow tires marked areas OK for students who had been cleared. Red tires were student-with-instructor only.

I would have the student land in one of these tire-marked areas to test their skills. After landing, they were required to throttle down and get out of the aircraft. Walking around the aircraft, they would look for any obstruction that might hamper their takeoff. Returning to the controls, they would hover to the best takeoff position and depart the area.

As a student, this was one of my favorite solo training exercises. I loved to explore the landing areas and look for artifacts lost in the Texas wilds.

A museum near Mineral Wells had cannon balls that the conquistadors had shot at the Indians when they came through this part of Texas. I would just stand awhile enjoying the view. The history of Texas is written in the cactus and mesquite.

I had hoped to find a cannon ball or some other lost item. Never did! I never even ran into a rattlesnake. I don't think they liked the noise of a landing helicopter.

Just southwest of Mineral Wells is a very large field at the bottom of a ridge line, surrounded on three sides by the Brazos River. Cutting across the field was a power line.

I would deliberately have my new students fly over the field on our first flight together. They had just come out of Intense Basic Flight Training, where engine failure procedures had been pounded into their hard, little military brains.

Their Basic flight instructors had required them to say, "Lower the collective, turn into the wind, call in my position, and land," parroting what they were doing at the time.

As they flew over the field, I turned off their engine. They immediately fell into primary mode, parroting their previous instructor's instructions.

Everything went well until I took the controls and asked, "Point to where you planned to land!" Each student would point to his chosen spot on the field.

Eyes got large and there would be a total loss for words. I set each one up so he was going to land right on top of a 10,000-volt power line.

I informed my students, "I don't want to hear you parrot again. I want you to do what you need to do: think, plan, and be able to survive on your own."

Secondary training was about thinking! Students can easily become instructor dependent. My job was to make sure they could make good split-second decisions, survive, and complete their mission.

In my 20 months as an instructor at Fort Wolters, I had the privilege of instructing 18 very intelligent, resourceful, and teachable young pilots. I passed all of them onto Fort Rucker, Alabama and to their futures as Army helicopter pilots. Much to my regret, I never saw or heard from any of them again.

I requested a one month "early out" from military service. I wanted to get back for the next semester at Western Baptist Bible College, which started in January of 1970.

Just as I received notification my early release had been approved, the military decided to release all the pilots in my graduation class. The war was drawing to its end and there was an abundance of helicopter pilots. Funding for the war was running out and extra pilots were expendable.

The military release was a month earlier than my "early out" request. I had to re-file and drop my "early out" or I would have to stay for the extra month. My friends all thought that was funny.

As time began running out, we made one last trip to the commissary. There were many boxes of canned foods added to the moving van, paid for by the good old United States Army. The van would take all our worldly possessions to my parents' home in Richmond, California; from there we would rent our own trailer to move us to Salem, where Western Baptist had moved during my military time.

As discharge time drew closer, we sold our mobile home, packed up, and prepared to leave.

In December of 1969, we left Mineral Wells for the last time. The Army was behind us and we looked forward to where God would lead us next.

CHAPTER FOURTEEN
50 YEARS LATER

My wonderful wife of 50 years and I returned from Kansas City, Missouri on May 2017, where we attended the 50th anniversary of my graduation from flight school.

I met Rob, Larry, and George the day we left California for Basic Training at Fort Polk, Louisiana. Our names were in alphabetical order, so the stage was set for our mutual military experience.

After completion of Basic Training and flight school, we received our orders for Vietnam. My orders assigned me to the 11th Armored Cavalry.

Rob was assigned to the 1st Infantry Division, where he was the commanding general's pilot. He and I had many opportunities to work together during our Vietnam tour. When he left Vietnam, he was assigned to Fort Wolters, Texas. His assignment was as the tactical officer for a training company. He left the military the same time I did.

Larry was assigned to a 1st Cavalry unit and spent three tours of duty in Vietnam. He was shot down at least once and was later promoted to captain. At the end of his last tour, he was assigned as the commanding officer of the 101st Airborne as they returned home. He stayed with that unit until his final discharge. He was in the military for seven years.

George was also assigned to a cavalry unit where he flew many types of helicopters and finally became a maintenance officer. He also spent 2½ tours in Vietnam. On his final mission, he was shot in the foot and was returned home for recovery and discharge.

I saw Rob twice in the last 50 years after we left the military; George sent me a letter several years after his return to let me know he had asked the Lord to be his savior. I had not seen or heard from Larry in 50 years.

Top to bottom, left to right: Rob, Larry, me, George

My wife was very concerned about attending the reunion. She knew no one except Rob, who had been in our wedding 49 years earlier. She was afraid she would have no one to talk to, and did not like the idea of spending her time around people drinking alcohol.

Peggy's concerns were relieved when she discovered both George's and Larry's wives were born-again believers. She spent hours talking with her new friends and praising the Lord for his many blessings. They both had the same concerns Peggy was wrestling with. We worship an awesome God!

I was thrilled to discover Larry had also been saved. We spent hours fellowshipping together and reviewing our lives with our old and new friends.

Rob's wife died of cancer several years ago. We are all concerned that Rob has not met the Lord as his savior, and are all praying for his salvation.

Same group…50 years earlier, before we left for Vietnam!

50th anniversary of flight school graduation; 102 left of original 300

In Loving Memory Of

Frederick H Elizondo

Killed in Action
Vietnam 1967

My Friend, My Flight School Roommate, and My Flying Partner

About Overboard Ministries

Overboard Books is the publishing arm of Overboard Ministries, whose mission is based on Matthew 14. In that chapter we find the familiar story of Jesus walking on water while His disciples were in a boat. It was the middle of the night, the water was choppy and Jesus freaked out His followers who thought He was a ghost. When they realized it was Him, Peter asked to come out to Him on the water, and he actually walked on top of the water like Jesus.

But what truly captivates me is the thought of the other eleven disciples who remained in the boat. I've often wondered how many of them questioned that move in the years to come? How many of them wished they hadn't stayed in the boat but had instead gone overboard with Peter? Overboard Ministries aims to help Christians get out of the boat and live life out on the water with Christ. We hope and pray that each book published by Overboard Ministries will stir believers to jump overboard and live life all-out for God, full of joy and free from the regret of "I wish I had…"

What we do
Overboard Ministries emerged in the Spring of 2011 as an umbrella ministry for several concepts my wife and I were developing. One of those concepts was a book ministry that would help other Christian authors get published. I experienced a lot of frustration while passing my first manuscript around. I kept getting rejection letters that were kindly written, but each echoed the same sentiment: "We love this book. If you were already a published author, we would love to publish it." They were nice letters, but that didn't make the rejection any easier or the logic less frustrating.

Out of that came the audacious idea to start our own "publishing company." I put that in quotes because I want people to know a couple of things. First of all, we're not a traditional publishing company like most people envision when they hear the name. We don't have a printing press in our garage, and we don't have a marketing team. Basically, we're a middle-man who absorbs most of the cost of publishing in order to help you get published, while making sure the majority of profits end up in your pocket, not ours.

Our desire is to keep costs to a bare minimum for each author. (As of this writing, there is only a minimal contract fee when your manuscript is accepted.) We provide resources and ideas to help authors work on marketing, while also providing the editor and graphic design artist at our expense. We subcontract out the printing, which speeds up the time it takes to move from final draft to bound book. Since we don't have much overhead we can keep our expenses low, allowing seasoned authors, or first-time authors like me, the opportunity to profit from their writing.

Contact us
If you are interested in other books or learning about other authors from Overboard Books, please visit our website at www.overboardministries.com and click on the "Store" link. If you are an author interested in publishing with us, please visit our site and check out the "Authors" tab. There you will find a wealth of information that will help you understand the publishing process and how we might be a good fit for you. If we're not a fit for you, we'll gladly share anything we've learned that might be helpful to you as you pursue publishing through other means.

Thank you
Thanks for supporting our work and ministry. If you believe this book was helpful to you, tell someone about it! Or better yet, buy them a copy of their own! We completely depend on word-of-mouth grassroots marketing to help spread the word about Overboard Ministries and its publications. Please share our website with others and encourage them to purchase the materials that will help them live "overboard" lives for Christ.

May God bless you as you grab the side of boat, take a deep breath... and jump onto the sea!

Joe Castañeda
Founder, Overboard Ministries

www.ingramcontent.com/pod-product-compliance
Lightning Source LLC
LaVergne TN
LVHW041321080426
835513LV00008B/547